the *NEW* *Los Angeles* *POETS*

Edited by
Jack Grapes

BOMBSHELTER PRESS
Los Angeles

Bombshelter Press books are distributed by Small Press Distribution (1784 Shattuck Ave., Berkeley, CA 94709).

Some of the poems in this anthology have appeared in various magazines, journals, and other publications including *Blue Unicorn, Poetry/LA, Tsunami, Sculpture Gardens Review, Ventura County Directory of Professional Women, Sea & Sand Anthlogy, Angels Gate Poetry Book, Snow Summits in the Sun, Pinchpenny, Caprice, Wordsworth's Socks, Footwork, Slant, CQ, Oread, Turnstile, Northland Press, Northern New England Review, Southern California Anthology, Z Miscellaneous, Shattersheet, Vol. No., Sucharnochee Review, Calyx, Wind, Lemon Fingers Emerge, Broomstick, Thirteen, Gramercy Review, Green's Magazine, Writer's West, Colorado North Review, Wind Literary Journal, South Dakota Review, A.K.A. Magazine, Pearl, Laurel Review, Seventeen, The Moment, Apalachee Quarterly, Bitterroot, Pulpsmith, Piedmont Literary Review, Black Bear, Yellow Magazine, Response, Embers, Tinderbox, St. Andrews Review, Amaryllis, Mind's Eye, Pandemonium, Archer, Impetus, Fiber Arts, Broomstick, Woman of Power,* and *Yellow Butterfly.*

the NEW Los Angeles POETS, edited by Jack Grapes
First Printing, January 1990

ISBN 0-941017-10-9
Library of Congress Catalogue Number: 86-73085

BOMBSHELTER PRESS
6421½ Orange Street
Los Angeles, CA 90048

INTRODUCTION

the NEW Los Angeles POETS! Good. Now that I've got your attention, I might as well admit that there's no such thing as a new Los Angeles poet. Becausé by the time he or she has been identified as such, there are twenty more lined up who are newer, and another ten who are newest.

The increased visibility of poetry in Los Angeles is part of a national phenomenon. Poetry's even come to television. Witness Bill Moyer's series *Voices & Visions,* and his more recent one on contemporary poets. Imagine that: Living Poets! Like the tree that falls in the forest, the spoken word is being heard. Inside the mind of a cynic beats the heart of an optimist — so I applaud this revival; perhaps it will save us.

L.A. is no longer just a city of actors. It's become a city of poets as well, and in many cases, the line between the two blurs. Are you an actor who writes poetry, or a poet who acts? Weren't the great poets all actors in some sense; and isn't the actor, who has to feed on his poor heart, a poet? Check out the *L.A. Times* Calendar listing of events for the week. There are poetry readings going on everywhere, several on any given night, from Laguna Beach to the Simi Valley, from Riverside to the San Gabriel Valley. New poetry magazines are springing up as I write this (mine included), and young poets caught with the fever are passionate with the possibility of their words. The doors may not be coming off the hinges, but they're swinging open and banging against the walls.

Not so twenty years ago. A small gathering of poets that used to meet in Venice once a week put out a modest book called *The Bridge,* and included the work of poets John Harris, S.S. Veri (Frances Dean Smith), and Joseph Hansen (author of the acclaimed Dave Brandstetter mysteries). In 1969 *The Bridge,* Volume 2 came out and added poets Gerda Penfold and Michael Dalburg. By that time, the Venice Poetry Workshop had begun meeting on Wednesday nights at Beyond Baroque in Venice. Fifteen to twenty of us sat in a circle of chairs and one old sofa in the small storefront on West Washington Bloulevard and read our poems aloud, got feedback, talkback, kickback, and punchback. It was a raucous bunch. Street people would stop and look in the window, come in and scrape up some spare change. Poets, huh? Sometimes, there'd be a little commotion, some action. The 60's were grinding to a close, and we were getting down to business. In 1971 a small anthology was published called *Venice Thirteen.* Some of the new poets featured were Luis Campos, Harry Northup, Dennis Holt, Barry Simons, Jane E. Newton, Lynn Shoemaker, and Anne Marie Ross. A new magazine of experimental writing came out, edited by George Drury Smith, founder of Beyond Baroque. Soon, there were monthly poetry readings. A constant group of twenty or thirty poets came every Friday along with a sprinkling of newcomers checking out the "scene." Such as it was. And that *was* the poetry scene in Los Angeles back then. We were a small family. Afterwards we went for coffee at the Lair (now a Cuban restaurant) or wine at the Brandywine to discuss poetry and gossip.

Then slowly things began to pick up. *Bachy* was born and lasted for a decade, 18 issues. Bill Mohr, who had worked on Bachy, started his own magazine, *Momentum.* In 1975 Michael Andrews and I hosted a series of readings in Hermosa Beach at the Alley Cat Restaurant, and published an anthology in 5 volumes which included all the new Los Angeles poets who had read there: Wanda Coleman, Kate Braverman, Harry Northup, Deena Metzger, Ron Koertge, Michael C. Ford, Eloise Klein Healy, Doraine Poretz, John Thomas, Bill Mohr, Bob Flanagan, and James Krusoe. Now we're the old Los Angeles poets.

In 1978 Bill Mohr published *The Streets Inside,* the first significant anthology of L.A. poets — 10 in number — followed seven years later by *Poetry Loves Poetry,* an anthology of 60 L.A. poets. In his wonderful introduction, he bemoaned the fact that he could have added another 20 if he'd had the funds.

Meanwhile, other poetry magazine were starting up, and other anthologies were being published. In 1981, Helen Friedland started *Poetry/LA;* that same year another Venice Poetry Workshop anthology came out, *Net Weight.* Other magazines included *Sulfur* and *Third Rail.* By 1984 poetry readings were being held all over the city. New magazines that have started in the last few years include *Blue Window, Tsunami, Verve, A.K.A., Pearl, Temblor, Southern California Anthology, Vol. No., Sculpture Gardens Review,* and *Issue.* I'm sure there are others in the wings waiting for the end of the overture.

In the last two years alone, two new anthologies have come out that I recommend highly: *Invocation L.A.: Urban Multicultural Poetry,* edited by Sesshu Foster, Michelle T. Clinton, and Naomi Quinonez; and *Snow Summits in the Sun,* edited by Blair Allen.

And now this one, which will be followed, I'm sure, by many others, with more new poets. I can't claim any kind of definitiveness here. These poets have had their work published in various magazines and journals, books and chapbooks. Some appear in print here for the first time.

Twenty years ago I wanted to know where the action was, and for awhile the action was confined to a small storefront on West Washington Boulevard in Venice. Now the action's everywhere. Put the anthologies and magazines and chapbooks and books in your knapsack. There'll be others to come. There's room for us all.

Jack Grapes
November, 1989

CONTENTS

3

5

The *NEW Los Angeles*
POETS

DOC

My daddy is beginning to look
Much like an old Indian,
Lean,
Leather-skinned,
Eyes black and vigorous.

But it is his hands that amaze me.
They are rotten.
Rotten from being washed
Over and over.

He washes his hands
Every time he cuts a cat open
Before he sticks his leathered finger
Into her belly,
Slipping her womb toward his knife,
Her blood pooling in his scars.
Then he washes again
As the poodle's breathing drops
To a shallow sucking noise.
Then the rough glove that is his own skin
Feels for the tumors
With the gentleness
Of a farmer judging his early peaches,
The same pressure,
The same sense of familiarity
Again the razor
Draws its line along the skin.
He wipes a spot of blood away
And sticks in his just-washed fingers,
Pulling the cancer to his knife,
Careful to feel deeper,
Knowing the tumor will have children.

He doesn't breathe himself,
But bends over the dog,
Weaves like a sailor
To the rhythms of its breathing.
"It was touch and go,"
My mother said on the phone last Sunday,
"An old dog,
But it looks like she'll pull through."

When I was little
There was always a dog asleep in a box
On the kitchen floor,

Waking at midnight with convulsions,
Dying from poison,
Snakebite or cyanide,
And he lay in the next room,
Straining against sleep,
Afraid to breathe
In case he miss a change in his patient's breathing.

Funny the things we remember from childhood.
I remember 1968
When the equine encephalitis epedimic hit.
From 4 a.m. 'til after midnight
Horse trailers lined up down old Highway 81,
Past the Highway Department,
Even past the Sigmore Shamrock station.
Next to the bag of needles and syringes
A bucket of water
So Daddy could wash his hands.

I'm not sure how many horses died,
But Daddy washed his hands once
For every horse in three counties.

If you wash your hands
Twenty times a day
For thirty-odd years,
Your hands will simply begin to rot from washing.
Or from being bitten —
Like the time a rabid sheep bit him on the hand.
That was the last time I went with him
To get his mid-belly rabies shot.
The last time...not the first, though.
We rode to school with him, me and Eddie.
On Wednesdays we'd stop at the old locker plant.
He'd take his big knife and purple government stamp
To check the giant sides of fresh-butchered beef.

Lots of things will rot your hands.
Kicks and being stepped on.
Rope burns and freezing weather.
Claws, teeth, hooves.
But soap is the harshest.

Last Sunday Mama said
Daddy is feeling tired these days,
That she's afraid he's going to retire...
That that will be the end of him.

But no I told her,
Lean old leathered-faced country men just like him
Populate the dominoe parlors
From Weir to Tulia

And sing off-key at the Swedish Methodist Church
On Wednesday nights and Sunday mornings
And hang around the auction barn at Jarrell
Just to worry over the price of beefstock
And maybe pick up a calf or two
To graze the pasture over winter.

Lean old Indian-looking men like Daddy
Hoe in their gardens each spring and summer,
Proud to kill a rattler in the okra.
I explained to her
How Daddy needs to breathe a little now,
To sleep a whole night through without listening,
To take some time to let his hands
Gather a little dirt
And heal.

IT OCCURS TO ME

It occurs to me
That to be human
Is to be the soul
of a dead bird
Who has sinned
An unnamable sin
Or was stupid
Or greedy.
We walk in confusion
Condemned to this odd hell
Anxious for meaning
Waiting to be reincarnated
As rain lilies
Or wild pigs
On some Pacific atoll.

I watch
As the gull leaves her nest.
I watch her circle above me,
Too stupid to envy her flight.
And when she is far out
Above the little breakers
Where the schools of minnows swim
I smash her eggs with my snout
And bury my nose in the yellow juice.

YOU AGAIN?

What mad artist
Created this sunset?
Did some dead post-impressionist,
Lonely for canvas,
Borrow God's sky?
Was that you again, Vincent,
Using windjet as paint brush,
To smear laudanum clouds
Against an indigo field?
This then must be
Your final masterpiece,
More fleeting even
Than your own life,
Equally violent,
Equally fine.

LIONHEARTED

for Charles Bukowski

I am a young woman
with the hands of an old man.
His mane, never golden
greys with the stains
of wine.

Pump heel deep in puke
if he makes me laugh
I'll drop him and
I can barely breathe
to keep from laughing.

ah young men
have no sense of
humour.
But if he had been a young man
he would have no
patience for me.

At the door we take the fall.
Laughing all the way down.

I am a bruised woman
with the eyes of an old man.
His shoes are worn,
at the track, his
buttons pop, are lost
underfoot. He smells brown.

He would take me for a
nurse, feel me up
at night, spit at me
in the day, strut in
his chair, nowhere to
go.

I steal his prescriptions.
Leave my drink in the flour
canister, appear on demand —
rosy cheeked, fair assed,
grimy, with unpaling innocence.

I am a young woman
chest as full as an old whore.

It happens. My toenails are painted
red. I cough to beat death.
He growls in snorts
sleeps awake, his tongue
slices his life to
shreads, reaches out
to my young life.

My life
takes us for lionhearted.

No one can crush us.

THE OKINAWA RADIO

Across the universe,

the stereo console blasts,
on afternoons at the McMahon's
and on the day the strange green car
arrived with a small green man
who wore his flat topped hat in the car
and carried with him the American flag
not folded square like a sheet but
folded in a triangle —
The Trinity, one held by nails to the wall
in the living room, but were any of them really there?

Then there was screaming,
screaming so loud that I couldn't hear
Paul sing, but Ringo's drums
pounded in my ears. After that
it was quiet, you're old enough to know better
cry baby cry,
while lying on the carpet
staring up at Tommy's face
on the top shelf of the glass case
surrounded by his ribbons and beret
in the light they never turned off.
Like John Kennedy's flame
the light they never turned off
so Tommy wouldn't have to sit
in the dark of his own living room
long after everyone else had gone to bed.

When my brother left
he took The Trinity with him
in his khaki duffle bag.
The Good Book, army issue,

but I saw The Holy Ghost follow
him to the plane.

He was there then, in that country
that wasn't America.
It looked all black and white
on television.
But he said it wasn't really.
It was green and yellow and blue and green
and the bushes grew thick, he said
like the poison banana bush in our backyard.
Imagine, hundreds of them, Chris
so that you can't see through them and
you don't know where you're going or
who is there with you.

In my brother's white album
there were pictures of nude soldiers
after a swim, with one guy's genitals
burned off with a cigarette.
And it was green and yellow
and blue and green, but
the ground was red.
And Jesus sat in the hot dirt
in one picture, in his eyes
you could see him thinking
why did i bother?
as he looked around himself at the whole mess.
And who the hell could blame him.

At Christmas,
my brother celebrated by walking outside
and exploding from both ends
because that's how sick he was,
from being away from home,
for being in that place,
and for being in Hell,
with The Ghost sprawled on the ground
his throat choking on the bloody dust
his lips bleeding, sick from something
for which he could find no cure.

The Beatles sang
tell me why
on the radio
the day at Norton Air Force Base
in the red and wood station wagon
we borrowed for the ride.
I stood with my dad and my other brother
trying not to breathe the jet exhaust
and waiting.

I was three inches taller then
so I could see higher through
the chain link fence.
My eyes followed the sun
and when the plane landed
it was still.

And then there was the screaming again.

The wounded soldiers leave first
supporting their stiff limbs on sticks.
Then the soldiers
who can walk without assistance.
The dead leave last.
My brother walked down the ramp
and he looked just like my brother,
followed by The Ghost who looked pale
and leaning on my brother walked,
both wounded and dead at the same time.

And although it wasn't quite Christmas again,
my brother brought us gifts.
He gave his younger brother binoculars
so he could see far and wide.
He gave his little sister the radio from Okinawa
so that she could listen to the Beatles.
He gave His savior back The Ghost,
who gave my father back
his first-born son.

FALL, AGAIN

the city is burning, again,
rumbling above the sea whose
splashes tease the blazing hills
stop short of easing the black pain
the trembling frames of houses about
to melt and ooze, slide down the face
of the belly of the mountain like
the sweat on my brow that burns my eyes
and draws my fingers to touch but not feel,

the pain in the distance
yelps the dog whose siren the police have stolen.

WALKING STRAIGHT INTO IT

In dreams I still see fire fighters
Combing the sides of Braintree Mountain
Balls of lantern light appear and disappear
Through the pine trees, through oak and birch
The fern
No outline of the mountain
Leans against a night sky
And I see nothing but the lights
Moving, always moving

Braintree Mountain
A thousand miles from the polio virus
Mother, my own bed
Across from the meadow of rock and low grass
Above White River
And the wasp nests of summer camp
From cabins on the lip of the meadow
We watch cycles of the mountain's life
And the path of Orion and the Dippers
As they pass overhead

Old Elijah Sims brings maple syrup
For our breakfast
Tells us stories of the Green Mountain Boys
And fires he fought on Braintree
Long before we are born
I imagine flames larger than the Merchandise Mart
Tall as the Palmolive Building
And high as the Lindbergh Beacon
Burning the trees and grasses
The honeysuckle vine
Leaving nothing but charcoal, nothing but ashes
Everywhere

Sometimes
Not certain, but afraid
We see wisps of smoke above the pines
Or rising over timberline on the western flank
If it's false alarm they come anyway
Invisible by day, lantern eyes at night
And I love these unknown people who prowl the mountain
Over the river from my flannel sheets
And bottom bunk bed

Blind Molly with me on her back
Won't hurry
Steps slowly through laurel and red clover
I look up at gray clouds that mask the dry woods
Where lightning strikes on Braintree Mountain

Shake the reins and cry, Run Blind Molly
But the rain can't wait
It falls from the mist down the mountain's side
Crosses White River, reaches the meadow
And with the wet earth smells coming to meet us
I let the steady rhythm of her hooves
Carry us straight into it

HANDS

Grandmother is old, she is frail
I am one hundred years
She says, tho only ninety-seven
Her fingers trace patterns on the lap robe
And she watches as they move
To the right, to the left
I am nervous, she says
I am nervous
Then her hands lie open
On her thighs
Palms touching the blue wool
She lifts them up, then down
Slowly, again and again
I sit in a chair
Close to the one that enfolds her
Cover her hands with mine
And feel the flutter of her nerves
Like a thousand butterflies
That struggle for release
From their cocoon

SUNSET AT LONG POND

My father's long fingers
Hold the brush again
They move across the canvas
Within their own rhythm
Paint the sun coral
As it goes down
Turn it to rust under the water
Against blue of night
Against the blue of Long Pond
Cold, deep
In the light that remains

This belongs to me, I tell him
It belongs to you, he finally agrees

In the studio at Wellfleet
At the edge of the dune

We smell the ocean
Through the open top
Of the dutch door
He steps back from the easel
To study this painting
That comes to me
When he dies

LAST CHILD

He says
I'm trying to grow up and be independent
And I don't need you to tell me this
And he takes a knife
That has a blade thick as twenty-two years
With a thousand words of advice
And a million and more questions
Carved into its handle
Cut through my umbilical cord
Releases me

KANSAS FOR THE WINTER

It's over for us at different times, that's all.
The young man puckers his moustache at me
Nuns slide trombones beneath their mufflers
All the while the altar boys are blue as clarinets
His fingers race me to sleep. Something about
he'll never leave me but someone else will.
His jowls are puffed dizzy as gills of blowfish en fac.
Whether I stay or go he mostly misses the feathers
on my forehead. It's the price
of stripes running down his arm.

Where'd that sailor get a nest around his head?
I get major sex attacks and leave notes
everywhere saying that I went to Kansas for the winter.
Looping my arm through the sailor's
I see we have a bad connection.
At least I'd be protected in a zoo
during the weeks when I became a cloud
I keep seeing street people wearing my clothes.
It never occurred to me until now that my mother left when I was born.
I just wanted to watch the sun without risking this much.

Since it amused me so, he'd spin five plates all at once.
Maybe I should have made a small trail
through the hair at the base of his spine.
Long after we were missing from each other
He'd look down and remember I was there.
Right there. Sucking his hip.
When I am beyond the landmarks of him, leaning into the needle
what I remember is the way he barbecues
perfectly balancing sweetness and the heat.

HE'LL BE BACK FOR MORE

What if it rains so hard
the seeds wash away, Mama?
Baby, this is L.A. It doesn't rain like that.

The woman he lived inside of now and then
turned into a page over time and
kept going out of control.
Women don't aspire to become these chapters.
With no intention of leaving peacefully,
she spits violence on his intuition
She thinks in maroon
and dreads what she doesn't know yet.
Women like her.

Don't mess with Texas, she thought.
He was heading towards the house
kicking the kneecaps piled in the yard.
Instead of what she was thinking, she said
let's take this one. He'll be back for more.

Mama, I'm gonna fall.
It's o.k., baby. Fall through yourself.
Everything is turning orange, Mama.
It's o.k., baby.   Fall.
                   Fall.
                   Fall into yourself.

HER NUMBERS IN MY HAND

They come in metal vats swarming like locusts.
These squads of children gone mad with their eyes open.
It is as if you could call one by name and this would stop.
The Contras give up their human name as a price to have the plague
move around them like water around an island.
Willing to kill a mother yours, you must never be anyone's son again before
you make her breasts hang like parched fruit.
Otherwise, what son can leave a mother this way
while a grandmother walks in circles in the plaza for the rest of her life
for her daughter. Nunca desaparecido. Daughters who are
young mothers do not disappear.

To be among the chosen defies translation in a world
where children pray to be invisible and will do anything to not be counted.
The geography of this disease is tatooed by numbers on her feet.
For a woman of the wherehouse there is a stench in her dreams.
The white doctors concur that this is a common odor preceding seizures
that she is unaware of and not to worry. I am her doctor now
holding her numbers in my hands, knowing she has been someone's grandmother.

The herds of madmen are dissecting the aorta of a whole people.
There was never enough air in the wherehouses or there in the death vat on wheels
where life is bruised beyond recognition even to the women who are the chant makers.
Rocking the babies before with songs to give a past,
they now take the sound out of infants by teaching a silence
that cannot be taught to babies. Hiding any sign of life
from the men trained as strike dogs to attack the life of people
who are in a rhythm that keeps erupting somewhere.
A brilliant virus is mutating again more clever than
the technology that swears by all the mistakes that must be made
to carry in another viral envelope and injected into humans with sticks and clubs
or anything that can break the skin.

These are the young butchers who grow up soldiers of fortune.
In the prisons there are truth tellers and those who've never heard it.
Baby dogs in houses of hiding just grow into mad dogs.
Worse to be a mad dog's mother. Worse than the maddest man himself,
whose mother walks in circles looking for a son she swears is missing.
He has been killed by his killing and she blinded by the sight of it.

I don't blame any mother anywhere for the round of shots
echoing from the park where her children are playing or
for thinking it would never be her daughter.
I don't blame any mother anywhere for never letting her only
remaining child out of her sight again. I act as if
I can want these children into someday playing a game and knowing it's a game,
that the girls who were raped by the boy squads who were their cousins
will be able to laugh again with a man.
Not while her grandmother walks in circles in a new country
afraid to leave the house no matter where she is.
She walks for the children who cannot answer when I ask
Who did this to you? Their memories have been poked out from behind.

The abuelita begs me to find the memory behind a small face
that will have to grow into her scars. Signatures in graffiti code scraped across a life.
Words never to be found to tell how the death squad tied her father's feet and dragged
        him,
cutting the vocal chords of a people and choking the voice of a girl.
Bombs in the distance yank out the middle of her life
Bombs that will follow her everywhere making the crater
that every mother will circle looking for her daughter.

The daughters are swept away in 1986 like reporters who see the truth
by the white mistakes that had to be made.
The children without tongues bear witness to it all
The children who have become the generation of scars
These daughters of the bombs without sound implode their past
as the generations made inconsolable by the coming of the death squad.
Their scars will blur every place with their trained silent throats.
They are still and alive with this slow virus pumping the record of death
through their blood. The grandmother moves like an oriborus coiled around
the mistakes that the white people say had to be made.

Too many names to remember between the one who killed and the ones who died.
The names keep changing of those who stood by. As if the scar faces can remember.
The children are everywhere looking until they grow up pacing in place as
the generation is hiding in search. Children become rats sold to coyotes
by grandmothers praying in circles. The children are hiding in sewers between
        countries,
their covered faces in tunnels too narrow to look back. The past has been stolen
in a mistake that the white people say had to be made.
A child is baptised nameless in a tunnel while a grandmother paces
with steps heavy enough for a generation. The girl pulls herself through the passage
away from the path of pacing where her scar face is on her grandmother's sign.

SOON WE WILL HAVE NO SECRETS

In Midtown Manhattan
I take my shirt off.
From my wheelchair I am
reaching back and up and up
for his neck to pull his head to my face

We are mudtramps laughing on land
Run out of time to ritualize this city's tension;
Not even, when the amputee next door
hung himself last night.

The village keeps on beaming with brick and vegetables
piled up and in and out. He is pushing me
through a change as indelible as cleavage.
No telling where we've been or
why we go where we go.
He becomes my legs.

I pass him a note on the Metroline
"Meet me in the dressing room"
where swift love presses back and forth
in a space too small to live part way.
It happened when I stopped daydreaming about
avocets wading on their stilts through the marsh
I was unwilling then; I am unable now to die of sureness.

Soon we will have no secrets.
A delay on the outbound Lincoln becomes
the story about his Uncle Mort
who disappeared when he was 10 and
Mort is still gone. We are the lucky ones
speaking scandals in a tunnel 25 years later
to cross into another life.

Maybe someday there will be traffic enough
on the inbound Holland to tell him
how I got this scar on my face.

Behind closed eyes I no longer see the longlegged birds
strutting in a slow procession to probe the wetlands.
In this bed we share sometimes and now
in my dreams I am walking again.

CRAIG BOREVITZ

MY TRIBE

1

I shoveled dirt
    on the casket I carried.
I heard the kaddish
    dozens of times
I listened to stories of Shanghai
    and recipes for blini.
I smiled at questions
    of when am I going back to school.
I explained my vegetarianism
    in front of unkosher meat.
I was told
    that I was known
    when I was just a baby

Be careful
Don't step on your grandfather's headstone.

2

There was a house filled with smoke
and a room filled with the cantor's voice.
there was food
(boy, was there food.)
there were drunks
and there were tears.
There was comfort
and laughter from
overdue reunions.
There was California's summer sun
and men in dark suits
with black kippahs.

3

Deanna sat on a pillow
        on the floor
and like us
she struggled to follow the rabbi
Everyone remembered something
    The Shema
    The Kaddish
    A Song
    When to bend the knee
only four of thirty
understood
    what was said
    or why we said it

But we still called
        every night
                for a week
                        we mumbled and mispronounced hebrew
Searching for traditions
        for guidance
Clinging to them
        for comfort
We wanted to understand more
        but it was enough
                to stand
                to face the candle
                and hear the prayers
                my grandfathers heard
It was enough
        to remember.

THEY WERE FRIENDS OF MINE

Maria tomalo!
        Es la vida tuya?
Amiga Carolina, arboles en las nubes,
        tira la basura
y sube la montana.

Bring home dreams
        too many to stuff in long days
Blue as black popcorn
        green as school chairs
Posed like a running train
        but quiet now
Cell blocks in mind
        blood on sister's back
Can't speak of brother
        remember thatched lives
In a tropical wind
        night passes
Go stare at suns that won't rise
        pray and hide knives
Mark dice
        cheat the sound out of steps
and dive where priests fear and monkeys swing
        always holding tight
The child you bear.

SPANISH CIVIL WAR

The Spanish Civil War
is not my life
walking down La Brea is

I am not the Spanish Civil War
listening to jazz
at the City
I am

The Spanish Civil War
was born before me
not the fear
that my girlfriend
has been hurt
that hits me
in the car
on my way home

A candlestick
sits on my table
I don't know
what sits
on the Spanish Civil War

I don't know
why the words
Spanish Civil War
keep coming out of me
it's remote
but
it's part of me

like the sliver of glass in my right middle finger

HER SOCKS

Are we eating her socks?
The big ones
    with no holes

No way man
    they tasted too good, too good
To be hers.

SAM SHEPARD CAME TO MY BEDROOM

Sam Shepard came to by bedroom wearing his hat and
boots. He waited in the doorway while I put on another
record from the early seventies, when singers sang
their own songs. "Shit," I said, "Sam, you look good,"
and he said, "I should, I'm making movies, I'm writing
and getting lots of money for it. I live with an
Academy Award nominee. I play cards all night and
wear this hat in New York City. No one thinks it's
bull and I'm still humble. What about you?" I told
him I practiced being in a western then put on lipstick.
He liked the color. It was pale and it made the
conversation about the absolute seem more intense. We
talked about the absolute best taste we ever ate and the
absolute worst weather in years. We got close. We got
real friendly. He asked if I would have his baby and
I said I didn't think that was such a good idea because
I would need him to stick around and I knew he couldn't.
He scratched his head and sort of swayed his long limbs
about, shrugged and gave me the coolest, hottest kiss for
understanding him. After he left I knew the real reason
why Sam Shepard and I couldn't make it.

I have lies to write that keep us apart.

THE SHADOW

So you press your idea
        it's the best one you have
against my fur coller
we dance
        it's just like the South Pacific
a hot night
you put your finger near my ear
I taste the afternoon game you played
it's still with you
the score never made an impression
the winner was cutting in
my favorite step was coming up
it had to be fast because you were moving too slow
        how else can the dance go on
        maybe the story is too long
        maybe
        who can tell
you have a shadow that never stops
it just stalks
it just walks into the room after you
sits down to cold beers and talks and talks

about the way light is a friend and the dark
takes the impression out of the ground after all
the taller it is the more moonlight it needs
the more soul is at the end of the run
    calm down I say to you as you question the texture of skin
and want to be in a city above sea level
you don't want to swim
I don't want to drown.

WALKING IN NEW YORK IN AUTUMN

Walking in New York in autumn
I understand his crisis
now
now that it is over
mine is just starting
thinking
am I worthy
am I lovely
    by nature
the crisp leaf
under my step
    what a crunch
    what a snap
Here on Central Park South
carriages are dancing into traffic
horses nod
at the switch blades flashing
against horse skins
dried and black
Buying peanuts for my nerves
    in the zoo
    in the cage
the monkey says
what about it?
are your worthy?
you sure look lovely
    he crunches
    he snaps
mops his lover's brow
squeezes her ass
laughs
I'm embarrassed
The musical clock chimes
Leaves tumble into my view
Walking fast
Walking East
Walking North
    where winter waits
    where the Egyptians rest
in turquoise shadow
trapped like mummies
we stood

       snapping our fingers
       crunching the facts
just like ancient times
just like this time
when I don't know
if I'm worthy or
if I'm lovely
       in the nature of fall
       in the season of walking

THINKIN' OF JIM

Thinkin' of Jim
He's here again
I talked about how he broke into my life
       blasted it apart
I recall all the lost moments spent on illusions
Some of those were called Jim

The buzz saw sounds
He makes a shelter
We hide beneath
He has a big smile
        a big heart
        a god time
  we dance in the spotlight
  a clumsy two step to a
  Talking Heads slow tune
  fast danced to Willy Nelson
  on the radio
  going to the desert on a six pack
  drinking drinking drinking and smoking
  we did choke on smoke and swallow
  warm beers as we rode towards
  Death Valley

I miss him
I miss Jim
He knew how to make
the time of his life
feel like mine.

I AM THE REAL BOB BROWN

what did my parents have in mind
when they gave me the name bob to go with brown?
did they want me to be one of the crowd?
did they want a name so dammed common
and easy to remember it would be a household word
potatoes or peanut butter, whole wheat bread or milk?
oh, what i wouldn't have given for a grandfather
named feodor or icktar, to be his junior
with a number to distinguish me
the third, or fifth, or even seventeenth,
i'll admit there was a time when i was proud
to have a baseball star or football hero
puff my name, but now i want to be unique
and have a name to match my differentness.
say what you may about me
when you hear my name, i want no doubt it's me
the one that likes big tits and has lots of kids
the one that looks like a leprechaun
and has a voice that sings.......
not like dylan thomas or walt whitman
or aimee cesaire.
i want to sound like who i am, bob brown
the one whose voice, teeth and tongue
sing common words
like brick and cunt and tree
and blood and flies and sweat.
i want to be as common as making love
i want to be love.
so there's nothing to do but embrace
my common name and use my voice to raise
bob brown to the level of the common man
i want to be the common man
and when i read my poetry
i want you to say, oh yea!
that is the voice of man speaking
created by God
but going his own distinct and idiosyncratic way
fucked up and full tilt
trying for all he's worth
to fill the vacuum that sucks around his name
bob..........brown............ man.

LEGEND IN A WHITE CADILLAC

this morning on the news
i heard about a woman
in a new cadillac

waiting for a parking place
outdone by a young man
in a red sports car
who said as he got out:
*that's what you can do
when you're young and agile.*
my sympathies
don't usually lie with
people driving cadillacs
but i was right there with her
in that hog of a car
my foot to the floor
ramming it into that red sport
saying as we got out
to look at the damage:
*that's what you can do
when you're old and rich.*

TRAPPER

the young trapper wanted to set
some traps on our land
hoping to collect a bounty
of thirty five dollars
a piece for coyote hides.
it's legal, he said
but i said no, thinking
he might catch a dog or child
or maybe even the spirit woman
of plum canyon
and then wouldn't there be
hell to pay
her with her foot in a trap
thinking it was set by me.
i've had enough trouble
without her circling our place
every night dragging
that clanking trap
the dogs going wild
like they do some nights
an owl moving to some other tree
like he did last fall
and the raging waters of the stream
washing our fences down
and flooding the barn
the way they did two years ago.
no, i know a bad thing when i see it
and i said no!
and i say it again
writing it here for anyone to see.
i don't want the wrong thing
getting caught in no trap.

not a poem

this is not a poem
so don't let your expectations
ruin it for you.
it is an orange balloon
and it carries me to
turquoise water
and tropic isles
to bevies of nude
native girls
lusting for me
or a yellow taxi cab
in new york city
darting in and out
of swanky clubs
to take me to luscious
women draped in furs
and smelling of love.
this is not a poem
it's a bagpipe
piping a procession
to an ancient gaelic
glen where i dance
with a bosomy irish lass
hot for my bones.
this is not a poem.
a poem would be free
and go where it wants.
this is not a poem
for i hold the reins
in my right hand
while my left hand
flies into the furry
muff of a white russian girl
warm and pink.
this is not a poem.
this is not a poem
not a poem not a poem.
if it were a poem
i wouldn't be
in this black maserati.
i'd by driving
my maroon station wagon
with the dents in the doors
my love by my side
heading for san pedro
or laguna beach
a bagful of macaroons
on the seat
and my hand on the
soft part of her leg.
that is a poem.

MY ROOT SYSTEM

You should stay in the South to have true Southern roots.
I didn't, yet my roots are there.
Daddy's buried there. I'm not ready when he dies.

I hate being thirteen.
I think I'm too old to cry,
I don't understand death. Not my Daddy's.

Daddy dies and Mother takes me to Africa.
I agree to go.
But it hurts.

I look at the clouds and feel I'm flying.
Flying back home
Back to my childhood.

Where I am on the edges
of a clique.
One of the originals.

Joined together in the Bang Bang Club
Till Beverly's boyfriend tells us to shorten it
to BBC.

We meet in Beverly's basement to have lemon squeezes.
You have to say something nice and something mean.
I go home to cry.

I take naps and sleep too long
When we have basketball games
So I won't have to sit on the end.

I think Nora is my best friend
Until she has a spend the night party
And leaves me out.

Going to Africa is a relief.
It gives me a new chance.
I bring Seventeen Magazine with me

To show to the high school girls
All six of them in a circle around my suitcase
Watching me unpack.

My roots are not in Africa.
It hurts Mother, because hers are.
I feel a freak in college.

I don't appreciate the attention,
I feel branded by it, and yet it seems a must.
I have to let it show in order to be known.

One reason I marry Bob is for his roots
Which seem stronger than mine.
I want them for my own.

I try to adopt his father.
It doesn't work.
It's hard to lose a father twice.

All Southerners are relatives.
We think Southern.
That means we feel guilty.

We feel love and hate all mixed up.
We're proud of feeling ashamed.
It makes us honest.

I lose my religion because Hitler killed the Jews
And find it when Martin Luther King, Jr. is buried.
I'm stunned by the forgiveness...the lack of hate.

I know I'm not part of it
But I still feel proud.
I sit in my California tract house and cry.

Our roots have always been at the surface here,
And yet we stay in that house
Seventeen years.

I'm trying to go down down with the roots, but I'm going nowhere.
The roots are getting shorter all the time.
I'm not sure where they're strongest anymore.

I think maybe the roots are just within me now
And Bob and Robby and Linda, and maybe just Bob,

And maybe just me.

GRANNY'S GLASSES

Granny looks funny without her glasses.
You can see the ridges where they usually go.
I don't feel like it's really Granny
When her eyes look naked.

But she keeps losing her glasses.
We're always looking for them.
After church yesterday, she leaves them by the pool.
She says it's cause I give her such a hard time.

I jump off the diving board just to show her
How I can dog paddle to the side.
But she jerks me out of the water
And says she'll spank the daylights out of me next time.

Sometimes when Granny gets too bossy,
I wish I could have a private city underneath my room.
I'll have the only key.
Maybe I'll let Granny in, maybe I won't.

I stay mad at Granny sometimes, but she never stays mad with me.
Maybe that's why I keep loving her.
Mama gets upset when I crawl over the pew in church
To sit with Granny. Mama says she's spoiling me.

Granny brings me surprises to play with during the sermon.
She has a ring she lets me turn to get the colors
From the stained glass windows in it.
I love to play with Granny's fingers.

Granny lets me sleep in her lap.
Mama does too, but Mama's lap is bony.
Granny's lap is big enough to get comfortable in.
She's soft all over.

She went home with Aunt Trudy last night.
I know she won't be back for her glasses
Till after I get home from school.
Maybe I can take them for Show and Tell.

Last week Beverly brought her daddy's telescope.
Mrs. Castle spent all day talking about it.
I bet Granny's glasses will be almost as good.
Granny won't mind if I'm careful.

Everybody's petting Beverly's rabbit.
Nobody cares about Granny's glasses.
Mrs. Castle says she'll get a carrot for the rabbit.
She thinks everything Beverly does is perfect.

I put on Granny's glasses and act like Mrs. Castle.
I know how to talk just like her.
Everybody's laughing. This is fun.

I can't take home broken glasses to Granny.
They're in a million pieces.
I tell Mrs. Castle they're mine
Granny doesn't use them any more.

If she knows I brought them without permission,
She'll send me to the principal.
The principal thinks I'm a good girl.
Everybody does. Beverly calls me Goody Goody Gumdrop.

Aunt Trudy's car's in the driveway.
That means I'll have to tell about the glasses.
Dudley Mitchell broke your glasses, Granny.
He grabbed them and he sat on them.

I shouldn't have taken them for Show and Tell
But I was being so careful.
Granny says it's awful what Dudley did.
Mama says it's just what she'd expect of Dudley Mitchell.

Granny's been looking at me all week.
She makes me feel like she can see through me.
She never says anything, though.
I dream about Granny and her glasses.

We have to go to the doctor to get Granny some new glasses.
She and Mama are talking all the way about the trouble
Dudley Mitchell gets into.
I'm glad you're not like Dudley, Mama says.

They made me come with them because
My shoes are getting holes in them.
We'll stop by the store
On the way home.

Granny says I look peaked
I probably need some Castor Oil.
I wonder
If she knows.

I made the best report card I've ever made.
I told Mama she didn't need to go for a conference.
Other parents don't, but Mama always does.
She's in talking with Mrs. Castle now.

Mama says I have to tell Granny what I did.
She wants to know why, why, why...
I'm sitting so close to the door, the handle's poking my ribs.
If I fell out, maybe she'd stop talking.

Granny makes me look at her.
She keeps pulling my face back up.
I expected better of you, she says.
I'd lots rather be spanked.

LIBERATION THEOLOGY

Someone brought his
stuffed dog
to church today

I asked the Monsignor what
church policy was in these matters

He said

As long as he doesn't
bark or bite

HORACE

I'm coming home after an endless day at the studio.
I was in the beginning, middle and the end of the script.
I entered first and exited last. Six a.m. to seven p.m.
And I get up at four.
As usual it was the time between the beginning and the
middle and the end
that sucked my blood and sapped my juices.
I drive Sunset and go to Fountain to finesse the traffic,
cut back to Sunset on La Cienega and coast home to Benedict.
I compliment myself on my cunning and comfort myself
with the green shade of the trees on Lexington and the thought
there is no nagging wife or chattering children to grapple with
at home.
I am wrapped in total euphoria as I drive up to the house
and get out of my car.

A giant German Shepherd sits in my front door.
We stare at each other.
I walk past 40 doors and gates guarded by dogs snarling at me.
The Hound of the Baskervilles--
its jaws dripping saliva and blood
and Cerberus his fifty heads grinning at me.
But suddenly the German Shepherd gets to its feet, stretches
and wags its tail
Welcoming yet reproving me for being late.
I read the dog tag on his neck. His name is Horace and he lives
in Holmby Hills.

He has a phone number.
I call it and a machine answers. So I leave my
address and the message I have Horace in my charge.
Horace is hungry and I give him a can of Kal Kan,
provender left from my dead bloodhound's provisions.
Some of my bloodhound's (he's been gone five years),

some spoor must remain to have drawn this dog to my
doorstep, drawn him to this least safe house on a
traffic choked street where there's a car totaled
every year for twelve years. A bloodhound's spoor is only
matched by the lion's whose dung is so insufferable it
is purchased to frighten deer and coyotes and racoons away.
Mine is the only house in the neighborhood free from
intruding wildlife.

But something else is at work here. Horace and
I understand this and we understand each other.
He shuns the kitchen and walks into the library and
sits down in front of the poetry--the classical section.
He doesn't move till the front door bell rings.
It is the dog's owner.
Horace rises, walks out the door and into a vast
Cadillac in my driveway.
The owner thanks me and as he drives away I see
Horace sitting bolt upright on the back seat
every inch the major poet.

THE GIRL

Suddenly
I meet her
we are both awkward strangers at the party
but
she makes it look easy
greets gargoyles, converses with druids
stoned to the gills in Milky Ways
oh the stars are out tonight stumbling over each other
while she dances as if she's skiing
bends in her dress to skirt the show
I can see it, hear its rustle as I look down at us
from above the air. No one knows we exist.

I knew a solemn girl who drove a Thunderbird painted tapioca and coated
in fur and feathers. A fuzzy car.
Not her she drives a black   .
and red suppository up hills and down daily
gaily yet not smiling either.
She sleeps curled up in a coil of garden hose
on my back porch all sleek and curvy animal in a silver cocoon
or on a beach whose sand slops over the edge
into an hourglass double-timed by a digital clock
whose toes and fingers are being manicured--a thankless
job when no hands or feet are showing. Are they buried in the sand?

Black caviar, blini and butter are mixed up
in her yellow hair which catches in my throat and as
she dives off the gangplank I am treading water
holding out my arms to catch her
and she slips through my arms to the bottom of
the blue pool my home is surrounded by

and I never find her again
except in lenses of
telescipes and binoculars or
in frosted windows

I felt exactly like this once before.
I am in Spain doing a movie long after the Civil War
having a for me dazzling luncheon as an invited extra man
at the home of the banker who had staked Franco.
One of Franco's daughters is at the table.
After lunch we pile ourselves into Ferraris and Daimlers
and race up to El Valle de Los Caidos
that huge cathedral carved out of mountain limestone
both tomb and monument for the fallen
of both sides during the Civil War.
The place is closed to the public for us
and we enter the limestone cavern
and one of the luncheon party sits down
at the great organ and plays jazz

Tonight I am an extra man again in Los Angeles for a dinner party at
the Bistro
but first right now we are at the County Art Museum
the "A Day in the Country" exhibit
is being closed to the public for two hours for our group
the Heads of the Museum are giving a party a private showing
we park on the Museum grounds and are searching vainly
for the private entrance. A legless girl in a wheelchair
is in the parking lot. "Can I help you?" she says.

A NIGHT AT THE OPERA

When I asked the cab driver in
Mexico City why he speeded up when
he came to intersections, he said
"Senor, that's where the accidents are."

BOOKS TO UCLA

I am donating my books to UCLA but they need indexing
Lois was doing the job but gave it up. She is taking
A course in thought transference and has ESP and a
Very psychic nature. As she went through the different authors she'd
Get these vibes just from handling the books. She got through
Beckett and Bellows and Burroughs with difficulty
Managed Durrell and Faulkner but when she hit
Gide she got ill. Graham Greene revived her but
Hemingway and Huxley did her in. She quit in the face of
Isherwood. Strange, there is a story if not a poem here.
The aura of the printed word reaches through the cover of the book
So the books of Alexandria burned. Big deal. Who died?
Here in my own room in my own home on my own time
At 10 o'clock at night I am as free as any man can be
It is too late for most people to call and I have no lines
To learn for tomorrow
Every selfish bone in my body rejoices and loneliness is antichrist
Each aesthete, hermit, medieval monk and solitary had it all
When they had books and were alone with them
So the books of Alexandria burned. Big deal. Who died?
I'll tell you who or who they tried to kill
The 10 million generations the first sovereign emperor of China dreamed
When he burned all books not dealing with
Agriculture, medicine or prognostication
The 6 million Jews almighty Hitler feared
When he first burned books in Berlin
So the books at Alexandria burned. Big deal. Who died?
Not them they are around me now
The Phoenix is alive and well. And so am I.

JANE AUTENRIETH CHAPMAN

DOWN ON SUNNYSIDE

they all slept in one bed
and stunk of urine.
Kenny Sigsby wore
khaki rubber boots
to school and never
took them off--
we begged him to--
laugh/sneer.
We knew he had no shoes.
Kenny picked his nose
and had gray skin.
He whipped the pants off
anyone at ciphering
and on the gravel playground
no one picked on old gray Kenny.
I felt sorry, sent a
Christmas card one year he
brought me nail polish
red as blood by Maybelline
signed, "Tiger."
Big tough mean gray tiger.
Lonely purr purr purr.

IN THESE DREAMS

listless as early air
I am already at the lake.

Here
in the anonymous water
I spend my day
escape the punishing heat
the relationship I can never right
with my mother.

Here
where only occasionally
someone drowns
I dilute my blistering need
learn to see
all things in swirls.

At mind's edge
these dreams cloy
like the vapor
of spent lilies.

TWELVE GLASS DOORS

"We don't remember the dream,
but the dream remembers us."
--Linda Pasten

Where hills fall over themselves
   in new green, a dozen doors--
all glass and billowing--
invite me in.
   The dream over, I lie waiting
unable to remember, wanting
   the dream to remember me,
      ask me to come to
that green place, leave this
   waking one where questions
      strangle each other
like thick vines.
   I want to go there, choose
      a door--any door, or
      all the doors--and enter
where everything is visible
and clear, where nothing is
   hidden, the only secrets
mere illusions, caused by
      tiny shafts of light
      refracted twelvefold
in the glass.

NOT THAT I'M MAKING A LIST

So what are we, 3/4 of the way--
not that I'm counting--it's just I
can't afford to sleep.
The leaves are coming down
in this hot wind
the door blew open
just like it was time to go.
Oh no, you say, 2/3 maybe, but
that's a different number.
O.K. Sure. But you remember Jerry,
his face swollen like a clock.
He raised one hand at 46
the nails black--
now Nora's walking into walls.
Not that I'm making a list.
Not that I'm worrying.
It's just that crazy sycamore
shedding in our pool.
One leaf's as big as any
dead man's hand.

NIGHT STORY

The darkness,
you insist from
blank instinct,
is a regret.
I say it's an ocean
we've taken to
concealing ourselves in.
Once you sifted
so softly
through promises,
you could have
touched the moon.
Now, escaping its
sickle edge,
you bleed
unusual words,
sprout thin shards
of wheat
from your veins.
And here, I climb
high up into a cedar
to stare at the sky.
My owl eyes tell me
the moon
is a white stone
filled with
empty pages.

DORI DENNING

MICHAEL

He parked the big grey Buick
on the wrong side of the street,
wore a London Fog
and carried flowers up my stairs.
With twinkles behind glasses
skin in his 20's and
pants too big
to hide the weight gain,
he slumped at the shoulders
too much for someone so young.

OUT THERE

My roots are buried
deep in this land
this earth of worms
twigs
grass
I work it for my life
it gives me life
and this open space
to look around and see
my brothers and sisters
are important to me
the most important
like this wind
this sky
this earth
hard and unforgiving

The rain comes
and scares me
thunder and lightning
can kill me if they try
but I won't let them
I run for cover
deep in the cellar
with homemade beer
and dampness

Stark sky
angled with electricity
sharp, jagged
hear me, will you
I am of this earth
but I respect the sky
I know the earth
I know the sky
but can't predict it

I wait til sundown
before I go to bed
I must have each ray of light
until the end
I'm up at dawn to see the sunrise
No time to waste
No time to waste

I am of the outdoors
I am nature
in plant and flower
tree and fruit
I know earth
nature
I know you
I love you

To have this til the end
is all I ask
it's all I ask to be outdoors
for the balance of my life
to breathe clear, fresh air
to feel hot wind
to see the sun every morning
and evening as it changes
as I change with it
growing like an old tree
finally bending
over
drying out
but out there
out there . . .

PARTY SMILE

What do I say
in the middle of the night
cold winter
red fingernails
soft lips
a quick passby in the hall
barely a glance
but a glassful of wine

HEADING TOWARD BURNOUT

She melts into the night
running at slow pace
never the only one
but alone
there's stillness on her shoulder
as she runs faster
a breeze across her cheek
to dry the sweat
only a little light
and running toward it
only a few more steps
until the falter
a little hurt on the pavement
blackness
recovery
blue-grey water
blue-grey sky
a hint of orange
and Venus on the rise

THE SCREEN DOOR

A stranger came to her house
and asked if he could mow the lawn

She used to dance in plastic shoes
on buzz-cut lawns
not to look for answers
but to pass the time

In less than an hour
I can do this lawn, he said.
she hadn't bothered to look down--
grass was so predictable

The stranger put his hand on the door

In plastic shoes
on coiffured lawns
lacquered ringlets on her head
she'd no idea how far
a fall could be

He walked to his truck
and took down the mower

From behind the screen
she called out to him
I'm a hatless tree
a two-pronged fork
picking sun from lint
I dream I walk in plastic shoes
on putting greens

The stranger didn't look up
He pressed his full weight
on the mower bars
and released the choke
The machine tore away the springtime growth
laid bare the winter roots.
Rotors blew the shattered blades
in all directions.
They fell in heaps
on rhododendrums
and cement.

HARD SONG

He complains of numbness in both arms
pain in his right shoulder
when he faces me in bed
He says he has a hard time breathing
if I watch him while he sleeps
He moves closer to the clock radio
I leave

He gets better

A month later
he comes to fix a broken window at my house
We work together
Through the pane
I watch him mouth words
of a country western song
I don't understand

He can't explain

He paints my porch grey
and the steps leading up to it, red
He wets my body with his tongue;
an elephant humping his dying mate.

ONE LEFT

He drove me to Fontana in the BMW
I still have the picture on the fridge
I'm by the trash cans,
the door is open,
I'm smiling,
about to get in the car,
the Italian shirt I'm wearing has pockets
that cover both my breasts

All the way to the hospital
he held my hand

When I came home
we ate without speaking
watched TV,
wore our clothes to bed
He held his breath
couldn't talk
I mourned the loss
. with mashed potatoes

That was three years ago.
My life is going so fast

He sold the BMW
and moved to Upland
with his new wife
I gave the shirt to Goodwill
went on a diet,
painted my house pink,
and bought a truck
Every six weeks
I drive to Fontana
in my white truck
to save
the other

SAT NAM (truth is my name)

The condition is doubt
that I can write,
lose weight,
fall in love.
I don't make sense when I talk on the phone
I want too much to be liked.
I'm down
on myself
the self
I'm forbidden to know
love and serve Him in this world
be happy with Him in heaven
not God within
not here on earth
Can I stop
childhood catechism
recited under my breath when I was seven
wanting knee hard to get it right
so Sister Paul might cup my chin
in her soft smelled-like-soap hand,
smile at me,
and tell me who I am.
Do I pretend to be a saint again,
lie awake at night dreaming
of Mother Gregory's tongue
touching mine,
feel safe in rooms
full of statues?
I called that me a lie
when my mother took me out of school
because my eyes were twitching
That's not the me I'm looking for
afraid to go in
my hips hurt
my stomach is full of wagging tongues
I press fingers to forehead
and do my affirmations

Some nights,
after warming up my feet
I dance a five minute gift
of no need to know
who I am

NORFOLK   NAIROBI   NEW YORK

My first husband was from Africa,
not really, but he liked to think so,
and it didn't make me no nevermind.

He looked so much like a Masai,
          his skin like shiny mahogany
          his eyes shiny zebra black
          his hair a black shiny mane
          that let the sun spike through
          in small notes
that he might as well have been from Africa
          and he spoke the language,
          the language of drums, humping one another,
          thumping lines of hollow sound
          for anyone who could sing
          to step across.

When we were married,
I looked like a pure white woman
in my long white dress,
baby's breath woven into my hair,
into my hands.
He stood, tall as Kenya,
in a robe, pure black and smooth,
with African beads,
the kind used for trading,
at his neck,
with sandals,
the kind used for walking
on his feet,
and he grinned at his prize,
taught all his life I was hands off,
and now he had me, even in photographs.
We said prayers from Nairobi,
from New York and Norfolk
and bowed our heads to the music he had written
          Morning, he called it,
          Morning across the Savannah,
          Morning in his own land.

And each and every morning, he'd wake
          trying to decide which he was
          African or Black or Musician.
He'd shave to Olatunji-the drums
          sliding the razor in jerky motions
          down his cheek.
He'd shake his big black ass to Taj Mahal,
          singing along in his high-pitched
          Baptist choir voice.
He'd stand in front of the mantle

conducting Mahler's First,
his face in rapture and lost.
One Saturday,
he was playing with the other drummers
in the quad   at Berkeley   by the fountain.
They'd worked up such a frenetic beat
with their fingers tapping and
palms rapping and sticks beating
and their bare feet banging out the rhythm,
that young girls, like dervishes, began
to take off their clothes.
I came up behind and kissed him on the cheek
and he flew into a rage.
He was African that day, couldn't I see?
He didn't want nobody knowin' he had hisself
a sassy white girl for a wife.

His drums would shimmer in dusk
and midnight and
I'd lie by his side,
wondering if the stars here
were the same stars that sung
in Mambasa. If they danced
to this same drum in Swahili land.
He would work me up into such a frenzy myself
that I would just sigh and moan
for the coming of it all

Another time, we were riding in the back seat
of this dude's big blue cadillac,
drivin' to party in Oakland,
over the bridge on 17,
and I was so used to hearing those drums
that when I shut my sky high eyes
and put my head back against the seat,
the rhythm of the tires became the drums
and I was black, Kikuyu,
in a village of thatched huts.
It was moonlight and the fire danced with me
and I stamped and swayed and clapped
and threw my head back   and back   and back
to that time with him, when he remembered
to be tender and to serenade the sun
coming up   in my ear.

I think of him   when I see someone
tall and black and shiny,
someone wearing trade beads
or carrying a drum.
I think about him smiling
and about the music   and the morning
and him, trying to decide who he was
          Norfolk, Nairobi, New York,
or just a drummer, beating his way through town,
to the top of the mountain,
where who didn't much matter,
it was how you layed her in the grass-yeah

THE AZTEC FINDS WHITTIER BLVD.

Hey Man
Since you been in East L.A.
things are different with us.
You act like a big macho
on the street corner,
snapping your fingers,
eyeing me up and down good,
making kissing noises
with your mouth.

"Hey baby," you say to me,
"Hey, you wanna go to the dance?"
"I'll pick you up at eight."
"You gonna be ready for me?"

Well, hey Baby,
that's the trouble here.
I am ready for you.
I am so ready I ache
and what do you do?

Take me out in your low-ridin' car
and feel me up
and drop me at the next corner,
eyeing me up and down,
telling me you'll see me later,
and eyeing me up and down
with promises of something better
Man, will you make me feel good
later, baby, later,
after you go home to your little mamacita,
and have us both in one day

Well, that's all I got is later.
Later, when I go home alone,
with my two kids, and my two dogs
and my two cats.
I take a shower, hold my breasts tight,
trying to remember what else
could happen to them
besides soap and water,
what could happen to them
in your mouth.
I sleep, with my hand caught
between my legs like
I'm holding a place for you.

My old man drifts in late,
makes like a statue in bed.
I turn over and turn to dreams instead,
but I am so pissed at you,
I don't even dream you
Instead, I dream this fine black dude.
He kisses me so deep,
his tongue reaches clear
to the back of my throat.

He pulls me real hard against him.
I like it.
He pulls me so close to him, I think
I'm gonna melt right onto him forever.
He wants me too-later.
I try to figure how
I'm gonna explain this to you.
Am I asking for a rumble?

Or just somebody to love
out of cars and out of street corners,
somebody who can love me
in broad daylight and in moonlight,
and that is not you.

It was better, man, when we
just lived in dreams,
when I met you in places
where nobody else could see us,
and you were this Aztec chief
and I was your queen
we could do anything there, man.

Now that you moved to East L.A.
You're just one of the boys.
You traded your feathers
for some cool shades
and a chevy.
You have done me in, man,
I mean you have wounded me deep.

AMEN

We are finished pasting pictures in scrapbooks,
making small talk about the times we didn't
but wished we did,   done with wondering
about what happened to old what's her name.

We are going to talk about something essential,
like the planets spinning out across the sky
on one silky thread   or the input of making love
with our eyes wide open in the rain.

We will not discuss politics.
We will not say remember again.

THE BALLAD OF THE LAST ABANDONMENT

Here the red woman of the lost horizon
cries "My life," "My life!"
On the patio of the gallery her sisters
do not understand their younger sister
so they talk in the tongues of their misunderstanding

Why do you hold the feet of death
with your lost innocence?
Why do you hold the stars? For what?
My God. One star.
You come on the last legs of the first green.
You are the transparent smoke of alcohol
in the black rooms of the soldiers of agony.
Go from us with the vanished corpses of your lines of worshipers.

The last flower of your mother, the contrary daughter of our heart,
go with the sorceress who raises up your brazen veil.
With the stretchers of the night around your beauty, pass from us.
The hand you hold out to your family has lost its power.
Your first son has grown a new mother.
She has devoured him from the foot to the head.
Many children has she.
No more have you a hold on any.
He is your lost son.
You may bring the sea to him in chests of tears —
you may as futilely bed the whole regiment
for all the good that it will do you, younger sister who has lost her son.

We turn in the sombre veils of the loneliness we feel for you all night.
No sentry watches for you from our windows as our favorite daughter
of the broken moonstone
pirouettes the circle of the mesa
with the sellers of the lost dominions of the Gaviotas,
sweeping the canyon for the missing horsemen,
combing the landscape for her lost darlings,
beautiful whore of the silent stars.

THE DANCE OF THE TERRIBLE MIDDLE

Caught in the terrible middle of the animal,
        in the white nerve of my sleeping grandfather,
with the whole circle of my blood
        and with the splendid sun of the baptism of our race,
            I go with the sign of night
in a straight line,
        eluding the contented star animals, breathing
            with the transformation of their high place.

The high mountains
are my prison,
        the fear of your love my punishment.
I occasionally give in to thoughts of you.
            The ghost of your spirit is in my center.
We are separate...in each of us
            is the house where both of us live.
In the table of your hair, in the locked room,
        to the living heart of the beast, we come
            for charity.

The sweet scent of reason
dances toward my middle self. It is both
splenddidly of the moon and equally
        of books.
But still this mongrel with its tail between its legs
                    howls a mortal solo
            of our spirit lives
    and our separate deaths.

        The rolling body of the star, my body spinning
    to the paradox
        of what I could believe in the faded ochre
            of the one truth of your friendship,
    the disparate truth of my father.

        All out of line, unparallel, my lover with his
six nights sleep, with five of his lives
            lost to this sleep.
He lives with three futures while
        I dance the tango of the terrible middle.

DARK, I AM DARK

I was always dark.
I can't
shake it,
just fold its corners under,
keep it down from
popping out at me like Bert
the night the bed fell in
and I got pregnant. Bang.
After he disappeared,
the night I saw him
in a Chinese restaurant,
he was with another girl
and I went out to sit in the car.
When they left, they waved at me.
Dark, I thought, this was very dark.
He pulled up beside me in the car and honked.
It wasn't dark yet.
It was getting darker.

I bled for a very long time.
I bled for months.
I bled clots the size of a baby's skull.
I bled in the museum   Boom   with the blood down my legs on
the marble with my father's
back in the wheelchair
back to me I ran
did my father see the blood
did he remember and
did he think?
What did he think?
I moved me off
to islands
where it rained
for a very long time.
I walked
in the rain
across rivers
to the scorpions in the trees
waiting for me
for my hand in the dark
against a tree
so I won't slip
burning dark
burning dark and hot
on fire my hand
and arm
finally everything
the tourniquet
the tourniquet
burned like the
venom
I was dark
it was dark in me
I wasn't only
I was both and all
and I didn't know how
to accept.

I rode a bike
a very long time
I rode a plane
and a car
and a landrover.
I drove everything
a very long time,
drawing toward but taking longer trips
to get further from.
Inching further.
Speeding away and
inching closer.
This is the world.
This is human.
This is life Everywhere.
We speed.
We inch.

MY MOTHER IS A BOTTOM DRAWER

In her we keep our pasts down low,
disorganized,
how we can stand them.

My father's gallstones
in a pink box
underneath her diaphragm.

The Andrews Sisters
still Boogie Woogie Bugling
ten years after the war is over.

Once, my mother caught me
on her Chenille bedspread
in the cool room off the kitchen.

It was sin
she said,
and made me wash my hands.

Now the sin is that I stop here on the surface,
afraid if I go any deeper
that I'll find the bottom missing.

In my fantasy she is a germ that grows in me
till she explodes and I'm left
plucking her like feathers from my hair.

YOU'D DO JOHN BELUSHI'S DEATH SCENE WITH SUCH INTEGRITY

for Jack Grapes

When they make the John Belushi movie
I see you playing the part,
sitting in front of a plate of pasta
with red meat sauce,
vermicelli in both hands.

Though your eyes are softer,
they grip, then skitter,
remind me of him.
The rest of you resembles him, too,
your height, nose, belly
the jokes, the excess.
With the right make-up it would be spooky.

I know Belushi wasn't a junkie
in the true sense of the word.
He liked linguini too much,
and women.

I notice women sit next to you
talented, pretty
and they want to have your baby.

John Belushi wasn't a well man.
The pathologist said he had a swollen brain.
I can't understand a swollen brain.
He also had a swollen heart.
That I can understand, like yours.

I've never seen you in a suit
and I bet Belushi never wore one
except in a movie,
but you'd act out his pain, his habit,
do his death scene exactly as it happened.

Your death will be more than a scene
in a Hollywood hotel room
dead, with that awful woman next to you.
You will die in some magnanimous act,
a thin beauty beside you.

Your eyes will skid about
as you tell the last joke.
There are no retakes here.
I tell you I'm dying.
I need the nourishment of absurdity,
the breath of laughter.
I can't survive
without feeding on the heart of a comic.

VICTIM

naked on the mexican shore
midnight   a boy and i
to make up for the last twenty years
i can't see
with the white blind of coming
i'm paralyzed with coming
and possibilities

police stand over us
with guns
the boy knows what to do
stuffs money in hands
cuffs, barrels, nostrils, ears
mouths

we run
i am airborne
i attach my gown to me
while i float above the sand

the stone wall•the hotel above
guests lean over and stare
in a dead-silent zone
i tear and climb
toward their chill watch
seem to fly

it's white again, sterile
i feel my sliced limbs
rub my imagination
over my wounds, my stitches
my broken face
my naked body,
the boy

YOU

made me go up
to the third floor-
daddy's bedroom in the loft
with my big new red rubber

ball
i wouldn't share
so you jailed me
at my birthday

parties
later i look for the
self in selfish
try bouncing free like a

ball
catch hold
put on red
just for

fun
false eyelashes
curly hairpieces
fishnet

dresses
go to singles dances
catch
someone to

ball
in my vw
vince sings italy
and a red

ferrari
i roll to a stop
i have three sons
and a dead husband

MOON

the moon gives a man
to a woman
drops run wild inside her
they are the stars falling
the man touches
the bottom of the sea

within the woman
moon water rises
descendant of fish
swimming in amnion
clinging like a pearl

red moon mocks the sun
steady as a stone
the woman bends
to the weight
of watr gourds
and a child curled
in her center

full moon
illuminates the woman
her body is a bell
she hears only one sound

RUTH FINESHRIBER

SPARRING AT SHADOWS

I write my poems with my father by my side,
bring him to class with me,
hide on the ceiling to ward off his testiness,
gather his necktie
pull on the silk to stifle his words
punch at his mouth
I am sparring with shadows
but the feeling is good.

I bring my father to class with me,
he is here now
standing in the corner, watching,
one eye closer than the other
judging what I say,
he is the ultimate critic
better than I could ever be
sharper, more caustic than a silo of lies
eating into my joys
building a tower of shame.

I go through life in hazes
sometimes slow and easy
often with a wild boar at my heels.
It is time to kick this baggage
Whaddaya say?
Cover the landscape with cactus breasts
sleeping mountains breathing in birth pains
writhing,
writhing.
It's all the same.

I carry Manhattan in my head
while outside wolves dance polka rings
around lamp posts
but I have seen the end of this film,
noted the credits.
How many of us can be a Stravinsky?
I am a snowpeak in a southern clime,
my desires meling into a bottle of Bailey's Irish Cream.
I carry Manhattan in my head
exchange limousines for gridlock ecstasy.
We make our faces as we go along,
the rust and web-like intrusions landmarks
of our fears
a map of our true selves.
The wounded eyes of Giuletta Massina quote
parts of myself
I am my father's daughter,
Like it or not.

LET IT GO

I know me
Better than anyone
Holding on to my gizzard
Not letting go
Leaning out of the window
Bellowing the March of the Toreadors
Ready to foul the bull.
I pick the scab off the sore
Cry my eyes to a boil
Patch my heart with salive
I'm good to the grain
Under the throb
Learning to love again.

Leave the image that holds you
Like a drowning calf caught in the undertow
Let it float away
Break up in all directions
Feed big and little paramecia
With peppered lintiness
The dregs of mental resuscitation.
Let it go
Before it wraps around you like an after-birth
Choking insensibility
Wringing it dry for the cleaning woman
To tidy up on Tuesday,
Replace it with another mess on Wednesday.
It is yours,
Do with it as you wish.
Hide it under the conch shell
inhale it until it oozes from your pores
Then, let it go.

I AM THE MUSIC

You deny me.
I am the pinch-boy
Who sits at your feet
Waiting for dandruff to drop
From your mouth
Bits and pieces of your life
Corsetted in Victorian trappings.
But clothes make the pirate, they say.
You brush your thinning locks it took
the barber forty minutes to arrange,
Bald pate shining like a discus
Life is a rehearsal,
A dance motif to an inner music
A far off beat.
The trick is to put the movement to the music
Then become the music.

NIGHTMARE

I walk down the hallway of a strange hotel
Watching a blind man deprived of his cane
Groping for some one or some thing.
His face is covered with a paste-like mask.
I look into his eyes.
They are the eyes of a man
Trapped in his carefully constructed
Annihilation chamber.
Under the mask lies blistering fear
Built up through the years
Layer upon layer
And under each layer
Another fear
One fear on top of the other
Married
Like a mille-feuille pastry.
I try to peel away the layers
But there are too many
I study the face once more
Seduced by its familiarity.
It is my face
My pain
My nightmare.

CHERI GIBSON

JOURNEYS BEYOND A SOLID CALIFORNIAN

we ran through shops like children
sampling cheesecake with smooth running pink syrup
trying on yellow and maroon beads you put in your
dark curling hair and
while you searched through suitcases
i surrounded myself in clothing, black and red
cotton decorated with triangles and circles
crossing one another. only men sizes.
i looked unhappily for one that would fit you when a
woman with blue hair and drooping lips
pulled me towards her, begging that i explain the designs to
her, i looked for you over the tops of racks and saw
your bouncing head running through aisles but my voice
didn't carry.
you are always drifting somewhere else to discover

i've read plato and marx and
i've eaten under pictures of picasso and wyeth,
i've staggered at reggae concerts and
drifted through underground clubs glowing under
fluorescent lights
but i've only seen the sunset on the west coast
and i don't know how to speak spanish
let alone japanese, although i always wanted to learn
and i've listened to you, while you don't explain
but you talk too fast

my breasts are too big, my mouth too small
my green eyes only green in anger and grey every other time
and my words inept from my mouth even while
stunning in my mind

i want to take japan away from you
the gardens, the language, the smooth movement of the people,
the orange, green and pink food that reflects the japanese
knowledge of beauty and hunger
i want to take away new york and its smoggy air
its crowded streets, the flavors of different cultures
on a single street, and its theatre and its towering people and
the connecticut retreats of ferns and slim roads and early
darkness and empty storefronts
of horses running through open back yards
and new mexico in the spring, in its blistering, in its
orangeness, in forgotten american heritage, in a
lost culture that lives and grows like a wasp

and still i struggle with the woman needing an answer
but you come
and explain the symbols with your hands

because they speak to you like clouds
and she walks away and i am left alone with you and your
language spanning worlds i will never see
as my fetus kicks me in the ribs and i remember
that i journey with her by proudly showing you
something you can never give me.

BLACK WALLED

the pastels of hidden cats
merge into the paleness of his skin.
i want to be lost there
surrounded by my imagination
where i can pretend
that his thigh overlapping
my hips would be a permanent fixture
and somehow we would grow together
despite either of our protests,

but the summer comes again
and he'll go.
i find the thought of missing him
before it happens
unbearable.
no more late night second looks
crowded into my single bed
before he goes home to the double bed
the soft wife
and cute kids
that annoy him
only when he's with me.

it makes no sense to pretend anymore

i'll give him back
his tooth brush, his comb
the flannel sheets,
the black walled bathroom
we splashed in lavender together.
and one more time i'll listen to him
dangle his promises before me
because they could not do more damage
than lying alone in wet sheets,
listening to the sound of his car
driving down my street
stopping at the traffic light
and waiting for the small tick of the turn
signal
as he turns
and if she doesn't know
about this wetness
how do they together
create their own?

the room is too hot for spring
the windows let in dust
i dream of cooking for him
and replacing the faces of his children
with children of our own

i am startled by my reflection
in the water boiling
brussel sprouts
can't believe my voice in my ears
turn the radio up loud
pretend that he's mine.

and again in the darkness
i spread him thin
slam his knees against my chin
watch the purple cirles grow
and his bones ache
they become my own
because i have none

1533

you don't have to worry about where the teacup came from
she still uses it to water the palm in the livingroom
the one with the dying branches; it reminds her of the house
where she couldn't get out of her bedroom window because unlike
the room on taurus place where it was cool green
because of the vera fern printed walls and hard wood floor and view of the
neighbor's fence,
this room had a slated window; she could only whisper
out the window in the middle of the night at her lovers
and she doesn't remember when they became so numerous
that sometimes when counting she would forget a few
only to slap herself later; the woman who could remember
the birthdate of the boy she liked in the sixth grade, who she had chased back
and forth playing an extended version of tag
and now she can't remember what day it is,
she only knows it's day because the shades don't keep the sun out
and the friends, they only come at night,
after they have left their day lives.
she leaves the phone off the hoook because
she hasn't got out of bed to call the
phone company to have it disconnected
and the ladnlord still comes by for the rent
but she leaves it under the mat.
she is still afraid that
she will go outside and then return
only to find herself in a room
walking back to the kitchen
for another cupful of water.

LISA GLATT

POEM FOR THE MAN IN WAIKIKI

I'ts 1:00 a.m. I'm 23 and a failure. Is that good?
I'm alone with a naked man in my bed. Dramarama is
on the radio singing marry me just marry me. Outside
mechanical crickets sing with their dark legs. Are they
horny or what? I think the Wild Kingdom guy or someone
said that. I don't remember. Now Morrisey is on, the
morbid genius from the Smiths singing about who will
swallow whom. Dramarama's singer wants a woman, Morrisey
wants a man and the crickets rub their parts together
with the same fucking song.

A tropical beauty is on my bed. I said I'd never touch him
again. There are his dark curls back on my pink pillow. I
want a cocktail. He's leaving for the islands in a couple
of days and I'm glad. He's part of a life I left, part that is
following me like thoughts of perfect weather. I miss warm
nights when all I needed was my own skin. These coats - at
first I was excited about them - oh coats and sweaters and
seasons. Now they're constricting, heavy, annoying. Nights
I drag myself through L.A. Out of place in my home town.
Out of place in my garments.

I look at the sleeping man and think, keep me alive, keep
me with you. Wanting the impossible. We are impossible.
We go together like Dramarama's singer and the insect
outside, like they could go off and share a life. Why
did I invite him here - why is he back in my blankets?
Thirsty I guess. A matter of tasting once again.

In Hawaii, the last time I tasted him. We are at Friday's
drinking and fighting about my red dress. I unbutton one
more button and drive myself home. I ignore my heart and
the red light. A cop pulls me over and gives me the test.
I touch my nose and walk the line pretty good but am crazy
and hysterical over the tropical beauty. The cop, convinced
I'm wasted, takes me in.

In jail, they throw a blond prostitute in with me. She has
on a white dress, is crying mascara and screaming her pimp
is a real fuckhead and why the fuck isn't he there yet. She
actually takes cocaine out of her bra and starts doing it right
there in the cell. I'm already scared to death, prison not
being a place I frequent, and here is this hysterical hooker
offering me drugs. I politely say, "No, are you crazy?"
Within minutes, she's sitting in the corner with her dress
hiked up and her hand playing between her thighs. She is
chanting, barely breathing and says, "No God no God."

There's a man in Waikiki that walks the streets, begging in his own way for food. He looks anorexic and wears a wooden sign around his neck. The word "Hungry" is carved into the sign. He walks through crowds of rich tourists with his brown cheeks sagging into his shoes and the sign bouncing on his chest.

From my cell, I see a cop enter with the sign around his own neck. His partner and the skinny man are behind him. This fleshy cop is laughing and so are the rest of the people here. Even the scum in the holding cell next to mine are laughing. Only the hooker in the corner, goes about her business, feeding herself.

Months later I'm sitting up in bed and the skinny man is crouched down on his knees beside me on the floor. He asks if he can please eat my arm. I say yes. The fat cop is next to me, his bald skull sweating on my pink pillow. He is my lover, this cop, this limbless, bloody cop. The skinny man asks if it is still ok for him to eat my arm. I tell him to go ahead. The prostitute comes through the radio singing No God. This is not a dream.

ONE WIFE'S PRAYER

He hits her and throws
his beer at the wall. A new
brown stain for her to clean.
Broken glass and bones
waiting in the carpet.

Later there is blood
on the sheets, where he
forces himself. His penis big
as a shoe and she
closes up like a box.

He shoots her
with a million seeds (tiny men
like him) and she hears
her mother in '59 broken
and bleeding into the sink.

Tonight
she prays
for a son born dead
or a daughter whose
hands, thighs and lips
will grow into
and love

woman.

SHOWER

I'm 23 and a child
when it comes to the dark
of blood, barstools, this parking garage.
It's midnight cold, the good smell of
the stoned and a purple cat screaming
in a bush. I'm outside, walking
toward the elevator and I think
of Dr. Watson's Social Pysch. class.
The woman in New York is stabbed
some 7000 times and her neighbors
pull the drapes, ignore her, like I ignore
the cat. I'm walking fast with my books tucked
under my jeans and I'm in the elevator now. A huge
man with a cut for a mouth that I've never seen
around here before kneels in the corner of the
box, watching numbers light and laughing. I remind
myself this is Newport Beach and yes there may
be republicans sucking the city blue but not
a lot of murder here and finally I'm inside
my door and surprised to find the apartment
moist and dark as a mouth. I sit my keys
on the invisible counter and from the floor
in the far corner of the room
a man says, "Ola." My body shrinks
into itself, rises to my shoulders. All the years
of 6 o'clock news and Grandma worried, mumbling
to the sink, come into my head.
I scream
like boiling water.

My roommate, Debra, from the same
corner chirps, "I'm sorry Lisa."
I feel in the black for the
phone someone to hold onto
when I realize it's not
a killer but a fucker
on my living room floor.

I think I am something part important
when I leave the workshop and Jack
says he loves me now that I forget
the poem and it is always back
to my room. Tonight still scared,
dumb at my desk — want to put the   alone
on paper. I remember
Mother that night. My skull hot
and wet. Her thirty year old face
worried, all her features gather
to the center. She shakes the thermometer
one last time — hard, gets up from my yellow
bed. Smoothing out her body's warm print
tucks me in.

Later that night I
hear her wailing and jump
from my bed, run to the hallway
to assure her I'll live. "Don't cry Mommy,"
and she says in words broken with
deep felt breaths, "I'm not crying Lisa
I'm laughing."

I stand in the black hall, listen
to him on the floral couch give
her a better baby. There in that
hall, dazed and dizzy, my first nibble
of death. In the kitchen
tonight's silverware, perfect and dry, at
stepfather's demand. Earlier I stood
at the sink, washing, drying, sweating, turning
blue inside. He named me, "Liar." Now
the giant knife, cold, in the good dark drawer.

Tonight all night Debra and the bigot
go at it. I want to pound the skinny wall,
shout, "I am alive damn it, awake
and forced to listen at 1:00 a.m." The bigot
yelling, "Shit shit oh shit" at the top
of his lungs. I turn the TV loud
louder. David Letterman and Stupid
Pet Tricks. The dog attacks his leg.
I get up, go to the shower, undress and
climb in. Want to drown their noise, myself,
the cat, blood from baby, the barstool down
the drain, the smell of nothing. Want fingers
of water on my back, tiny edible ponds
on my breasts
to save my life.

ERIK GOETZE

THE REGIONAL OFFICES OF THE DOUBLE

I was sanding down the shingle beach because I like it fine
I was grasping the bruised lizard to my life's dusty turquoise pebble,
I was mining a charred buzzard of land for the golden dogs parked on their
    tails
When Major Tom spits out a sunset and it goes clicking on the damp rocks
    Meaning at eleven,
"Roast a saguaro until the dice call you Carlos   the maze"
because abbeys of chrome file the subdivision of jaguars on a bicycle of
    precision
so that the complete spectator can feast upon the Chevy posture forever.

Exhaling the air of my filed down blade,
the Martyr Man spends a feeling that was bought
Inhaling evenly, the artist child sucks up an astral body
slicing open the elegant sturgeon of my barbed wire skull.

Later that night I fell through my TV into a doubt mine filled with jagged
    cows
breathing little bubbles filled with stock option dogs running loose
a professional mistake to spill that silk,
but a bumblebee suit doth deliver me to a birth in heaven
while my stomach smells another world coming on
A grim leg wearing a tie in the walletless swamp of Big Boys from Bob's
sterilizes my future with nary a bark or howl
but the guacamole was excellent.

Take this and buzzword it back: "You're worse that Elvis Yoghurt"
but rogues don't bitch about the thighs of plaid cucumbers
that binary in the night at the regional offices of the double
Arriving in every nostril, the jaded beer can rise up and new york me
with a canyon of copper teeth gulleyed with bumps
Succulent windmills usher us into the arms of varnished rattles
we must now go to jail for the sins of our cars

Like no dog before, I come home to a God instead of a father.
Take these knobs of freedom and Red the night long;
of thorns, of girls in skirts sitting on concrete ledges at noon,
of tombs proclaiming hatchet parlors for Satan,
of women foolishly giving their thighs to leopards;
these things happen when this word processor prattles backwards
into another surreal evening of raving sanity.

All she fancied is celestial quality,
like ball-point-pen jazz sizzling horned toads on the sun,
or the dusk in the spear as it hotels my nose
Let the flame thrower of satire in me calm the nest of squirming baby
    numbers
and make me arithmetic baby until I hark

evenly and free of burning roosters or bit parts in heaven.
just mind the Dogs stuck to your velcro star bucket
and penetrate that atrium in her devout growling marble of ruined men
like the Erik outside the screaming door glutting a freeway
and planets need Einstein T-shirts pickled with cataract jars
and elbows driving my face mad while the good times ride the grasshoppers all
the way to New Jersey.

This morning strange sleep murdered a fermenting brain
in this oblong room God is a parrot on the ceiling
building me into the Rudolf Hess of love, confined to my own homeland
to pace down through the carpet hours
producing potatoes from the hundreds of Dr Scholl's padded brain insets
piled up behind my courtesy
to control the speed limits of pain
out there in the footnote to my couch female
little buttons of her ear were scrambled
like black rocks dilated into egg madness
The green ice cream cuts that coke glass until it departs
stay with her please I grovel
and eventually die in the bibliography.

THAT MUNICH SENSATION

It all seems too easy maintaining the appearance of a normal life
like everyone else when inside I know it's all wrong, all rotten
no matter how good it looks on the outside.
People here believe in the surface, it's more tangible than the past
which no one knows about.

These girls were lucky when they looked at me so hard and got nothing in
return.

The could have gotten 20 centuries of German Gotterdammerungs hurled in
their face.

What is it in the German soul that brought these mountains of bitter defeats
and humiliating failures upon me
and even though I'm not stainless German,

I know what it is to grow up with the bier stein on the mantle
and the chair with the bloodspots on it
and to make a dozen stollen in the grandparents' kitchen at Christmas
and all that damned sauerkraut and to have such a great plan
and it's all lost in a crazy tornado of historical accidents and coalitions.

What does Hitler have to do with this melancholy anyway?
He's just the singular reason not to be a German in this century

For now to be proud of the piece of Berlin in me
puts all of World War II in my eye . . .
The gray blemish of a past that came bad.

THE ERIK OUTSIDE THE DOOR

I can't wait to start drinking the hot coffee sitting next to me
it seems that this will be my only company tonight
if I hold true to my decision to stop seeing her.
The evening ahead seems clean like a white sheet of paper, or linen
She doesn't make it easy with her saran wrap conversation
that goes on and on about trying to be a better person
I should have made that speech with the last five women
who went out with me, but went on to better things
and I needed them in gluts, like stars need Einstein
but here she comes, again into my mind, a turbulent cataract
no man-made dam could hold back, no engineer could contend with
the rain in her New York; the weather in her eyes
perhaps a poet, a musician, a genius, an actor, a novelist, a painter
could play the right note and her sun would flash on the water
taming it with a touch
like the one I gave her at the Farmer's Market
on another day of no preference for where to go
I took her to the same shaded patio where my grandfather had touched me
with the extensive sum of 35 cents
and I wanted the poem I wrote her to make a difference
but the truth is most of my poems simply disappeared
after she read them; evaporation by confusion
or a second or third tongue and more heartless bullshit
from the son of an angry man
that's the metropolis of my expreience squarely on the page
for everyone to walk down the lines and swallow or spit out
in the gutter or the toilet, that's where these words will end up
and if it's a shallow place to be, and this heart a shoal
it's because nothing   scared me like
the screaming in the middle of a freeway at midnight
or the fifth in a series of all-night monologues parked in my car
or the sugar jar winging across my living room towards me
or an elbox smashing into my face as I drove down Westwood Blvd
or a hot hand thrashing my boyhood bottom for the evil I didn't do
or the spittle on my father's lips as he raised his voice
                and at the same time lifted his large arm in threat

or seeing myself rend the front door right out from the plaster
                of my own place in the chained gang of being locked out
Fuck you she says Fuck you with a capital "F"
at that point the memories of the good times go off fucking to New Jersey
and

fancy that-this is the same kind of love I had at home . . .
She asks me these days how I can live without love.

MOTHER MOLD

The newspaper headlines are about
Margaret Thatcher and I don't care.
I've come to the last donut hole in the box
and only regret that this indulgence
can't go on and on.
According to all accounts,
I need to pay myself back.
I get into such a martyred crouch,
such a twisted shape.
I wonder how I ever got to be
the mother of so many.
I barely do what must be done
and that with resentment.

For once I put a little love
into the cornbread
and then they will only eat it
by force.
The after-dinner beach trip
is cancelled
by the Eat-Your-Beans showdown.

I curse about the Legos in the bed.
When my mother swore,
I thought, "You don't hear
what you're sayinng.
It can't be what you mean."
Now my mouth screams the same words.
I do hear it, I don't mean it,
but it's the shape of my anger.
I pour it into this mold
this mother mold
this martyr mold
this metal and bitter mold;
not surprising that my children
are allergic
to mold
and dust
and the crumbs that I offer.

I poison the water that we drink.
I dig up the murdered goldfish we bury.
I drown any hopes that float to the surface.
I turn kisses into dental surgery
without the novocaine.
I turn bedtime stories into
stiffly belted white jackets.

I turn picnics in the park into
poison pen letters.
I turn hemlines into burned hair.
I turn games of Sorry into
you-can-never-win.
I turn cookie recipes into
lead weights tied around their necks.
I turn again.

I turn around.
I call their names out the door.
Iturn on the television set.
I check under thier beds.
I look down the bathtub drain.
I turn all the pockets inside out and
they're not there.

I bake a cake and trim it
with pink rosetttes and hearts and
magic candles that can't be blown out
and hang streamers over the table.
I twist my hair into a neat bun
and wear a cameo pin at my throat.
I cut out paper dolls.
I sit back and wait
for another chance.

NOT FOR THE ALBUM

I look at the snapshots,
twenty-four frozen moments,
but this one
freezes me now.
The most recent trip
to Golden, Colorado,
to visit our oldest son.
The Marriott Hotel room
that always looks the same,
January, May, October.
You are sitting
on the edge of the bed
watching him eat breakfast,
pancakes from room service,
heavy on the syrup.
I stare at your face
in the photograph.

Anyone else
might think you had a headache
or that you
were remembering the day
your father died.
Or someone else

might think you were a
starving man
forced to watch
another person eating.

But I know
that expression.
I can read
that posture.
Only I can't believe
I took the picture.
I created this.
I put this one away quickly
and show you
the other photos,
twenty-three shots of the naked baby
washing his toy car.

SCARLET SOAP BOX

All you people jogging day and night on San Vicente Boulevard,
I am speaking to you from a long line of official trees,
Coral trees, planted, pruned and fertilized by the city.

The trees with deep coral gifts appearing on naked branches in February,
    have something to say to us.

A single petal is a flower in itself, a violent tooth,
A brilliant keepsake of the depths of passion,
A message unsurpassable at any speed.

Never mind the rain that chills you.
Never mind the cars that honk off-color.
Never mind the strands of roots that cross your path and tangle in your
    shoelaces.
Disregard odd black starlings jeering at you from the telephone wires.
Disregard wandering hub caps that entreat you to invent a new causeway.

Bring all your attention to the heart of the matter.
The color you collect in your hand, waiting at stoplights.

This is the color that brings each one of you to the end of the boulevard.
This is the color that gives you Ocean Avenue and salt spray to enhance your
    deep breathing.
This is the color that unites those of you in leotards with those of you in
    sweatsuits, the exhibitionist with the utilitarian.
This is the color that unites the fast walkers with the athletes in training,
    grandfathers pacing their dogs with housewives burning off calories
    of resentment.

This color permeates every reason.
This color transcends what you can ever accomplish alone.
This color is your destiny, your essence, your blood.

VALERIE JOHNS

SPIKE
(The Baseball Poem)

In the summer Sundays with first stage alerts
make the air into mushrooom soup
We'd drag ourselves out of bed and roll down the hill
to the Thugdome at Fairfax High.
Tom came from a party with his cut-offs and mitt
and changed on the bench

It was my up
the score was tied
there were two men down
the infield moved in
they knew a girl couldn't pull it out

Neal was hungover at third
wondering why we played so early
wondering why he'd picked somebody up at the Rainbow
that he'd never wake up next to.
So I Threw The Bitch Out, he'd crow
but he didn't look happy
waiting for me to fly out to short.
Be The Ball, cracked the pitcher
Bilecky yelled One Of These Days
She's Gonna Surprise You Guys

Bilecky felt responsible for Terry
beating me up
he wanted me to do good
I mean, the guy was his friend

Cameron's first pitch was high.
Wait It Out, Wait For Your Pitch.
The next one was mine,
I forgot about falling away
into the rain and mud in the hills
I connected and ran
Tom came out of the dust on first
throwing me over his shoulder
I screamed and got loose
and took off for second.
The Thugs yelled Hold Up and I did.
When I stopped, I was winded
Neal came home to score and everybody was yelling
JB howled, I Told You She'd Do It
but I was remembering
grade school, when I was captain
not because the boys thought I was cute.

I was a real ball player
and I whacked it over their heads
every time at bat
and I could've beaten up anybody
who said different

the smog hung low over Fairfax
and old Jewish people went by going to Canter's
it was Sunday and I was twenty-six
I'd hit a double
and that was good enough.

and I couldn't do it anymore
not now
It wasn't that I was out practice
or playing with people out of my league
it just seemed like everybody was playing hardball
and smiling, calling it slow pitch
and I had bruises all over.

The shortstop said Who Beat You Up?
Tell Me Who Did It and I'll Kill Him.
I said I Did Some Quaaludes,
Fell Down a Flight of Stairs
He laughed.
He believed it.

Kevin whacked a home run into left field
and I scored
and we cheered

It was easier to play ball
when we were just playing
and not living out some metaphor
or even
just getting
even

COMPOSITION

I worry about important things.
Like whether to cut his pajamas into shreds
or burn them or mail them to his office
or wear them to his sister's house
the next time I go over to play with her kid.
Been composing this confrontation for weeks
forgetting till I go through my closet
looking for clean socks
and find the New Rochelle Athletic Dept. t-shirt
and WHAM
back into my past, skipping now and travel to my future:
It's a great fight.
Slinging curses and How Could Yous

and slapping him--just for effect —
after he says I Still Love You
Love Me? You Fucked Me, I scream
and look at my watch
it's now, not then
there's no fight, never will be.
Come back.
It's enemy territory beyond today.

I surrender, which is a good thing,
I was going to kill him with the gun
that mysteriously appeared
since if you bring out an unmentioned gun
in a scene that's giving you trouble
everyone is so relieved to be excited
they never ask where the gun came from.
If anyone asked me where the gun came from
I'd have to lie, which is easy. I've done it for 30 years.
I'd say, very slick and cool,
that I copped it on Venice Beach
from a junkie
who stole it from a very famous actor
who hit the skids
on cocaine
It's a famous gun
it killed an Oscar winning actor
in an Oscar winning movie

but I don't lie anymore

THOMAS BROS. GUIDE TO HELL

You make a right on Sunset
and then another right
When it dead-ends you make a left and
get to the fork where you can either go left,
right, or sort of straight and you go sort of straight,
at least you do if you want to get there,
then you go right and look for a pack of dogs

big dogs
dogs that you hear about in passing
dogs that won't be locked up
and foam at the mouth
dogs that hump on playgrounds at recess
and steal children from playpens
while their mothers talk on the phone

dogs that were never puppies, who eat cats and birds
and don't spit out the bones
mangy stinky mad dogs, always black,
black with no spots

beasts that won't circle before lying down
and never even sleep, unblinking, howling at the moon
and giving me nightmares
dogs that live in caves, labyrinths
offspring of gods and hookers
they corner me on my bicycle
slobbering on my legs
oh, god, these dogs are big.

CO.

In an alleyway
In Denver, Co.
The buildings are mostly old,
Two, three story dwellings
Made of brick and mortar.
From one comes a soft, light rock sound,
From another the scraping of steel on stone,
The whistles and hoots of carpenters,
A muffled Christopher Cross.

To my right is a small, garden patch edged
By a cheap wire fence which leans in
Towards a burned mass of broad dropping leaves.
Beyond the scorched hands stand a row of thick
Tomato plants. That is all.
Perhaps the white stone house is a church
Now unused. The air bites at my skin.
But I am saved by chills
By an equally hungry sun.

I am here for no reason whatsoever.
I want to photograph the plain image.

The white aspen line Magnolia.
The gold penny leaves don't glitter as much,
The sun and wind raped some splendor
For winter's arrival. Soon
The aspen will be matchsticks.
I write spasmodically
From stiff thoughts to the aspen
To my conversation with Mark
And back to this paper again.

I think the aspen are elven trees
Faded from gold.
The stone above us is steep, bold and committed.
It makes winter look shy.
My voice rings with the day.
Smooth, resonant, seasonal, swiftly changing.
I want it to be brilliant and preserved
Like a color photograph.

TIGER LILY SKY

Sidled against the clapping rosebud and African tiger lily
  she roars, sugared bright by lemon rays.

Truly I am upside down for a garden snake
dangling with my tale caught on the invisible rim of a distant star.
Laughing, lounging, spritewitted and creative by birthright,
Slithering down into brown soil, biting thought,
building fertile waves of the future.
   Say it's dry, dry cold climate here.
Say love is dessert at lonesome end of layered tunnel.
Still all alone in my head. Still in the garden of eden.

I cannot complain squirmed around metallics and stone.

Living on earth this side of the milkyway
marked by galaxy pastures steeped in glowing sonics.
I bring every dream recorded with me to this green eclipse,
and every test as well.
   I conceive the day's and the night's glory by trial.

MA

I just woke up mesmerized, happy, vacant.
I just woke up after vacationing from daylight.
The sky is white and spits at my windows.
And my feet are heavy with sprouted stones.
I just woke up and I'm sneezing rain out of my nose.

I'm awake now and formed again.

I just woke up from Mark's great boyish chest
Where I lay in the protected silence of my sheets
Mother is making me warm green comfort to breathe
She is always here when I feel like this to make right what hurts
Everywhere.
I want to say I'm lucky because at whatever age I am
When I need her she finds me and

Lies healing beneath my feet.

CHANEL

First I put thunder all over,
I then applied quartz
To articulate the contours.
In the midsection
I spread twilight
To add height.
And last the cobalt, which
Opens the innermost corner.

Why I sit here on the floor, tired at midnight
Straining to see (against the glare of a 100 watt bulb),
My face in a dusty mirror,
Is because I have this desire to make a costly black
Plastic box containing French baked colored domes
Convince me that I am beautiful.
To rescue my mind.

I've never liked
The funny lump of cartilege that shows inside my right nostril;
Or the scar beneath my right eye;
My pale skin that never turns golden brown in summer;
And my square jutting jaw.
My complexion isn't right, I always have pimples
And they've left small, red marks all over my skin;
If only my hair were naturally curly and not fine and limp.
My last two permanents burned my hair and
I had to cut it all off.
Even my legs are too short•I wish for long slender legs
Without jelly thighs that wiggle.

All the things that the girls have
In the cosmetic commercials
And in the glamour magazines
I want.

Really I want to love what I am.

THE QUESTIONS A DAUGHTER MIGHT ASK HER MOTHER

We drove to San Diego last summer,
my mother, me and everything we both
had just been through.
We took my father's sickness with us,
Danny and the woman he was living with,
And when speaking of men, crying of men,
we spoke the same language.

She never reached out to touch
me as we drove.
She felt the tightness of my throat,
Cried my tears for me.
And I felt her mother pain.

We talked about all the women
bound to dining room tables,
hands shackled by cups
filled with coffee,
speech filled with apology.

And she told me she was sorry
for teaching me
how to tip-toe on my feelings,
keeping them unexposed and
out of danger.
She told me she is afraid,
as she watches me
from the corner of her eye.
My head is bent
and I am turned off
from being shut-down
for too long.

And I told her, I am tired
of the miles,
And I wonder how long
I will go
before I turn around
or give up.
And will I ever stop
counting the days,
or stop remembering,
if it's Monday, or May, or summer,
or, if it's even my life at all.

REGGAE MAN

Another bar - bang, bang.
It was another night,
a different kind of time.
A reggae man swayed front to back.
I missed Wooley and Rose
so much that night.
That reggae man, that dancing man,
Wooley for me.
And now here - tonight the dance
floor is empty.
The bass is just as loud,
but no one is dancing.
Someone should put on the lights.
Guitars are better with the lights on.
Love is better with the lights on.
Small wonder.

FUNCTION

Fourteen of order   in or out
                      time's up
cat smile   eyes too close
             set in diamonds   trust
stacked words   in peanut crunch
table holding foot   glass refrigerator
peaches don't care to be exposed
                      poets do
                             how old do you think
                             she is?
care not to care   high triangling
penny green plants   make sewer   stew state   steel state
stem rust
do you think she wads her wafers?
tough

WHAT I DID AS A CHILD

When I was a child,
I spent most of my time,
in my room with the door closed,
putting secrets into books with dates and locks,
tying sweaters around my head, rosary beads around my waist.
Oh daddy, I will never forget the look on your face,
when I walked through my door,
a nun.

PASSAGE

In the language of motors
I hear voices speaking ancient tongues
that live in ruins near the equator
Ospreys and grey whales lurk in the baja
I saw it on T.V.
A pageantry of flukeless whales seized by the outboard
    and chopped
ospreys wheeling regurgitate love for their young
Movement in the lagoon pushes
     all my flat vantage into clay
     or the promise of small, vapid
     figures, counting the visits,
     tight in their johnnies and
     tiny octopi spew out of egg sacks
     like viscous sails
Everything in the ocean looks like sperm
     or a dubious sexual appendage
I can't think about any other possibilities
when all that fucking and dying is going on
I can't imagine loving something so much
     I would vomit
     or by duty hold my talons clenched
When the scratch comes
I'll throw telephone tables and bloody the sconces
    of old, gentle money
My mother will breathe mint into my hair
     and forgive me my darkness
     and I'll wheel and roll through the house
     three floors to set every bicycle whirring
I will believe the August storms that I sat out on the porch
     with cocoa and saltines
thinking murder to be the sport of kings
Orange and the trees were on fire that year
up and down the street
Odd light changes ripped the leaves away
The gutter filled with Fall and ran
through a dream of real chestnuts
It was a summer
tricked with lightning and heavy plumage
that bore me into youth

I moved through the fire without a sound
without an inkling
that I would ever know any drama but this
or that blankets would sour
     and we would store the chaiselounge with hoops and winepress
     lost to the license plates numbering the Depression

In wooden splinters I hammered a song
of purpose to the silver dell
where I never went but fishscales wound through
my dreams like stars or a final desert
At night the float was willow
      cupped each hand a bright azalea
         dripping nectar and rust through stamens ravaged by spring
Now, the heavy August bound us
Clouds limned the moon with an open hand
and I saw for the first light
how it would be
my breasts, dark and bouyant
my skin, fissured and tall
How the earth was come to measure me
and the night relished me
and the supple pool cast me out on currents of eel grass
      that spelled my journey with each undulation
What ends is your childhood
and the brave suburban love of parents
fed out in arcs of acceleration
A greater lawn grows away
and every trickster beckons
Young and laughing, I follow

POET LAMENTING

"Stall for Rent," says a sign painted in a shaky hand
the kind of printing a horse might do with a brush
   held between his teeth
"Stall for Rent"
Bruce can't stop laughing
He sings along
A horse is a horse
of course, of course
It must be hard to act with a horse, he says
and I have to agree
although Wilbur seems to handle it
What I want to know
is how they get the horse to lipsync so perfectly
and what does the horse get out of this, anyway?
a byline
Mr Ed, starring as himself
Big deal
I'm starring as myself
I lipsync pretty well
But when I can't write I'm nothing

Learn to rhyme, Bruce says
Study classical form, he says
Discipline yourself to work as the masters did
Great, I think

Bird thou never wert
I read him "Love is Still Possible in this Junky World"
He likes it
and says the lesson I should learn
is to stay on one subject
He never liked my surreal stuff
the path of least resistance, he calls it
too many words, he says
quit jerking off
I'm scared he's right
but one subject is like cleaning the house
I feel the weight of my limits
one subject, one story
I can't do it
unless it's a T.V. show
and someone else has done all the work

You know, Picasso was a complete master of the basics
before he went abstract, Bruces says
Jack already told us that, I say
Even a jazz pianist has to know all about basic melody
before he can improvise, he says
Yeah, I say
You're too close-minded You gotta try new things Do you
    want everything to end up sounding the same? he says
Do you want to come teach the frigging class? I say

Jesus
Everyone's a goddam poet

A LIFE OF BUSY SWINGING DOORS

On the street today
some guy said
Miss, can I talk to you
just one minute
I said no
I'm going to work
and he said,
Fuck you, he said
Fuck you
and I went through the swinging doors

I am a woman
blessed with prosperity
my skin is veiny, translucent, culpable
my children will say to me
How could you live then
knowing what you knew
about the rest of the world
You didn't do a thing

And I'll tell them, kids, I'll say
It was a life of busy swinging doors
we lived by a map of England
tacked to the wall
It was a first world of whiteness
I didn't give it a thought or a good goddam
and if I did
it was too big
my hands were too small

Still now I won't believe that the fur will fall
or that our long sleep was bought at the point of a gun
that my centuries were a mold for blood

It just seems an old story
something we all know

AND FOREVER

The man on TV is 32
He's grown but he had a lobotomy
and now he's eight, they say
and forever

Imagine, eight forever

RECALL

for Jack Spicer and *Billy the Kid - IX*

Spicer came to dinner
said we could be
his brothers
and sisters
always have
clean sheets
lots of gravy
chickens pecking in the yard
dreams living forever
inside one another.
Spicer's dream aches in me
like small bones
despairing.
In the shadow of the pines
I hear roots grow
secret stones click together.
I think back
to buttons speaking in a cookie tin
blind man's bluff
hide-and-go-seek disguises.
I know the elephant's foot
half full of umbrellas
is a true story.
The dream is living.
Like someone canoeing on a small lake, I
keep rowing.

ONE-HALF OF HISTORY

Her names are not
remembered. Her story
lives in cave paintings
tiny fine stitches
harmonies and legends.

Always
there were dragons
then sailing ships
iron horses, flying machines
and many battles.

Men carved their names
in stone
in honor of their wars.
They wrote of one
another

while she stitched together
whole tribes
sewing up wounds
and comforters
with fierce precision.

The future will suggest
she evolved
from man's imagination
but her legends speak
line for line of life.

ONCE REMOVED

for Lenore

It's just that all
the little things are not so little
your fingers pinching
picking at air
eyes staring at things
no one can see
your sounds neither
sobs nor laughter
as the morphine drips
all day all night while
bones break unseen
unheard among
veins and vessels
where cells collide
and the words there are are
backwards or lost as
memories now are backwards
when thirty years ago
is yesterday without pain
and every dream excites us
enough to make us chase it
all day all night
we ran and now
it's hard to breathe
watching you
pinch the air
and pinch
the air.

IN THE DARK

These shadows inspire
prayer suggest something
is waiting.
They move
in and out of sight
disappearing
when I look and
when I don't
gathering in corners
like dust or ashes.
They could be cousins
ignored too long
or undreamt dreams.
The real threat
is a voice
that says
if I go exploring
I might not come back.

CLEANING THE BLACKBOARD

I return to your dusty face each day
to wipe away yesterday's words
and careful equations.

If anyone asked why,
I'd say I do it because I dream
the process of learning will last forever
because I dream you have absorbed it all
and I return to you each day
the way people return to friends.

I'd say, "It's this--that I trust you,
the way a boy, fishing at the edge of the lake,
trusts his line will vibrate--
trusts the fish will strike,
or the way a girl, baking bread,
trusts the yeast will rise."

I'd say, "It's this anticipation--to learn
to trust the dream, to let the dream
change us when it ends."

BARBARA LOMBARDO

NGO

Sometimes when China is mentioned
I hear in my mind Grace Lee's voice:
Nay ho ma?
Nay gong gwong-jau-wa-ma?
Nay djiu hai bindo-a?

My supervisor as a surgical secretary
she was recruited by Stanford students
to prep them for Cantonese census taking.

I took my lunch at nine to join the group,
groped hard for sounds my throat had never tried--
the "ng" of *ngo* to be swallowed like pride.
"Ngo siu seng,"...My small, insignificant name is:

I hoped not to be identified
with the only other Anglo, his goal in life
to join the CIA as an agent in Mainland China.

I was proud at the final banquet
to prefer *fijee* to fork,
to eat all my *bahk fahn*,
unlike most *sik-sik* Anglos
who eat their meat and leave their rice.

When the chatter changed from food to
"Would you allow your daughter
to marry a *haole*"?
I waited for the earth to swallow me
like the insignificant syllable for self.

Translations:
Ngo -- I
Nay ho ma? -- How are you?
Nay gong gwong-jau-wa-ma? -- Do you speak Cantonese?
Nay djiu hai bindo-a? -- Where do you live?
Ngo siu seng -- My small (insignificant) name is
Fijee -- chopsticks
Bahk fahn -- steamed rice
Sik-sik -- picky eater (literally one who knows how to eat)

FOR ALL YOU *ESES* FROM BELMONT HIGH SUMMER OF 58

C'mon, *ese*, none of that dangling your *huevos*
through the impudent holes
in your royal blue sweat pants.

I mean, man, are you *puto* or *papa*?

I want to whiff,
I want to scratch and sniff,
I want to obliterate literate history with you
in one turn of the screw.

The only one before you who ever cooked dinner for me
what's his name?
hamburger in the electric frypan prelude

I didn't want to intrude on his bowling team
but had to explain
that being Jewish
I couldn't expurgate it all with Hail Mary's

and I was more accustomed to sucking the necks
of chickens than cocks.
 That's how the *culo* cools
when you're raised on bagels and lox.

THE EYES HAVE IT

Four-and-a-half
and Marc knows about eyes
already.

A strange grownup speaks to him
and he folds himself in half
lowering his eyes from her sight.

I want to reach down and unfold him,
make him tall and free
because I never was.

Those first glasses when I was 11.
Bad enough to change a world that was soft
like the Monet calendars my mother liked
into sharp-edged realism.

But to look like that
into the privacy of other souls
and know they could see into mine.

I moved into the company of books
where my eyes were always down
and kept them there through high school.

Once in U.S. History, Armando Martinez,
a graduating senior with a Roller Derby scholarship,
caught me looking up.

In the same breath he asked,
would I go to the Sweethearts' Ball with him,
and was I pregnant?

LONGER NIGHTS

We make love and I fantasy myself
an earth goddess
being shaped into perfections
by Bill's touch.
For once there is time
for us to stay holding each other
until he sleeps,
and I think, "this must be written down,"
and I get up and write:

> *How the Earth was Made*
>
> *Young and smooth she met him,*
> *and he was older and wiser than time,*
> *knowing how to mold her mountains*
> *with caresses*
> *and tease the alluvial fluids*
> *from her until the universe*
> *trembled with their merging.*

Afterwards I laugh at my production,
sit beside Bill drinking a warm bottle of beer
while the house sleeps.
We should have longer nights.
I curl myself around his warmth,
put my lips into the soft hairs on his shoulder
that were not there when he was 21
and I was 18.

BETWEEN CALLS

You call collect, the third time
in an hour: *Mother, it's the size
of a walnut, maybe two
But it's not cancer*

I hold on while you speak
Spanish to a woman
at the clinic, *uno, dos*
inserting dimes for her
because she wants to use the other
phone, and doesn't know how much
it costs to make a call

Thirty dolars, you say, *or maybe
they'll do it for nothing
since I don't work,
I don't own property*

I think of the times
I left you
your first day of school
the boat speeding me
toward Venice, the sinking city
your voice calling *Mother*

Now you are a woman
Yet you call me in the middle
of the night, in the middle
of a meal: the plea
always life-or-death: *Now
Help me now*

And I run to you,
crying *Yes, yes, I'm coming
I'm coming.* But even when
I reach you, even when I say
I'm here, even when I touch your hand

Your fingers slip through mine
Your eyes stare blankly, you
look at me and say,
*Why are you here?
Why have you come?*

TWO DAYS HOME FROM A VISIT TO MY FATHER

Your wife has sent me home
with books on cheese and housekeeping.
And I have eaten the last bar of chocolate,
the last of five you gave me,
that I kept cold all the way from Tucson
to San Diego, through Yuma
and a hundred and eight degrees.
I followed your highways--10 to 8 to 6--
instead of my own because you told me
to avoid Phoenix, and we have such
little time left to submit
to each other's small wishes.

THE HAPPY FAMILY SITS FOR ITS PORTRAIT

On the mantle Daddy is upside-down,
balancing on one finger. He is waving
an old letter and singing "White Christmas."

Outside, the Italian artist leers
at the window. Calls *Mama*. Plaintively.
The cocker spaniel serves tea

from an ivory tray strapped to her back.
Asks me to spell my name backwards.
Cathleen. Neelhtac. In the doorway

feathers, crystal beads, Charleston
music and Grandmother, carrying one cardboard
box inside another: mother unfolds

herself from the smallest box in the center.
Sphinx-mother, ready to disappear beneath
a cardboard flap. Bekins could cart her away

with dishes wrapped in newsprint and who
whould be the wiser? From a hole in the ceiling
an old yelllowed rope snakes

to the floor. My brother climbs down,
straight off the cover of Backpacker
Magazine. My husband rows across the carpet

from the west coast of Connemara.
"Wrong house," he says, and rows away.

POEM FOUND ON DECEMBER 9TH
WHILE LOOKING UNDER THE LETTER *I*
IN THE INDEX TO
THE SELECTED POEMS OF FRANK O'HARA

I am not a painter. I am a poet.
I am sober and industrious
I am very happy to be here at the Villa Huegel
I cannot possibly think of you

I cough a lot (sinus?) so I
I don't know as I get
        what D.H. Lawrence is driving at
I don't know if you doubt it

I don't remember anything of then,
        down there around the magnolias
I have a terrible age and I part
I know so much

I picked up a leaf
I ran through the snow like a young Czarevich!
I think a lot about
I think of you

I wanted to be sure to reach you
I'm getting tired of not wearing underwear
I'm having a real day of it
I'm not going to cry all the time

FOURTEEN LINES FOR AN ANNIVERSARY

So much to resolve. The next day at the shop
in Boulder, ready to buy the mask I'd seen through
the window the night before. Up close it was

not a wolf. A coyote, contemporary, *hecha en
Mexico*, studded with upholstery tacks. What
I need is not another mask. Or a Kiowa

dance wand. What I need is your bones
in mine, not counting on stars or waiting
to see whatever it is one waits for. We are

only human, a man and a woman with toothbrushes
and hope. My skin is the only miracle
for today, and the fact, the *given*, that you

will appear at our weekday door in five hours
calling, as always, *Anybody home?*

SHIRLEY LOVE

TOMORROW AT NOON

I will meet the virgin in person.
Many things are plausible
and to be believed or not
depending on what they stand next to.
She will be standing by the STOP sign
at Aspenwall, under the large "S"
which is god's name.
From a chain at her waist
the letter "T" will hang
like a key over her womb.
I will not ask her about this or
if "O" is the wrath of god
or only the sound of a door opening.
She will be holding the last letter
in her arms and offer it to me
wrapped in a cloth.
It is a gesture familiar to women.
She will be there only as long
as it takes to see her.
She is no more elusive
than any other neighbor.

THE GEOMETRY OF INNOCENCE

Draw a circle over here around Julie and me.
Then a five pointed star. Get it? For his
head and arms and legs. The devil thinks
his shadow's falling out of heaven. The devil
is a fool. A foolish devil begets flies.
Now sprinkle us with salt. Close your eyes,
Julie and say, "salt, salt, lick the plate,
never cry if the devil's late." Stand up so
the devil can see you. All squashed down,
he'll think you're a toad and you know what
he does to toads. That's a good circle.
You're good at circles. Now get in. Step
high over the star so your shadow won't get
stuck. We'll all hold hands. Hand over hand
like a braided ring. But tuck your thumbs
under. The devil hates thumbs. Mad in the head
and mad in the limbs, won't get to heaven
on a book of hymns. Now we all close our eyes.
When I count to ten, yell, "spit, spin, devil's
in," and spit as far as you can. Ready?

THE INNOCENCE OF GEOMETRY

Flora Lou discovered Persia
when we were fifteen.
Omar bending over a girl
with good teeth.
She brought the book to geometry
drew poppies and weeping willows
on her homework.
In her gold earrings and purple sweater
she looked like the girl in the *Rubaiyat*.
Every day she owned more of Persia.

Mr. Morgan didn't say anything
about the poppies
but he noticed Flora Lou.
He loaned her his orange and black
copy of *Flatland*. A book
of many dimensions.
Men were triangles and women
straight lines made invisible
by turning endways till they were
only a dot.

Flora Lou wore black triangle earrings
and a narrow skirt.
She stayed after school to talk
about being two-dimensional.
In the hall she'd whip out
a piece of paper and draw a line.
Imagine this is the whole world,
she'd say.

But *Flatland* turned ominous.
Women were needle-sharp
and men were afraid.
They resorted to law.
Women were required to become visible
again. They were executed for sneezing.

Flora Lou tied up her hair
with a gold drapery cord.
She went back to doodling.
She drew vine leaves around
Caesar's tomb and Omar's
seven-ringed cup and
the white hand of Moses.
For the final, we constructed
an isosceles triangle.
Flora Lou drew a rose made entirely
of dots.

TO THINK ABOUT SOMETHING
doesn't mean you have to be serious
all the time. Like edges.
I'd like to write about them
so it's clear once and for all
edges make the difference.
Where the trees end and the sand begins.
Or the cat. I can see by its edges
it's coming over here. First its
whiskers are along one edge, then
its right ear (which was on the other
side before) then the corner of one
eye, until it turns its head and the eye
goes over to the other side
but I can still see plenty of edge
so I know it's a cat. When it sits down
I see how space has this cat-shaped hole
which goes along everywhere the cat does
and I start noticing how everything
I see is an edge to something else. And
what I can't see, like the inside of the cat,
would have to become an outside edge
for me to see it. But I don't like
imagining the cat cut open, so I imagine
a glass cat with a red bubble where
its heart would be and how I can look
past the edge into the middle and out
the other side. All this time, Jennifer
is saying the states and their capitals
and she missed Montpelier, so Montpelier
is the edge of what I'm thinking about cats,
which makes me wonder if thoughts
actually have edges you can go over.
By now I'm really enjoying this and I want
to talk to somebody so I find Bruce,
who's shaving, which is perfect because
I can point out to him how strange it is
that his face is one long continuous
edge. No it isn't, he says. So I
take the razor away from him to show him
how the flat part is also an edge. Everybody
knows what the razor's edge is, he says.
Well, I tell him, what people know has nothing
to do with this and I read him the quote
from *Scientific American* about perception.
Even the water in the sink, I say. Just look
how it has an edge. But he drops a sponge
in the sink and soaks it up. Sometimes
it's impossible to have an ordinary conversation.

CONTENT
(after Dylan Thomas)

When I was a gangly girl and a bit
and tightly tucked in the church's hold,
(signed the dear wanton, flying from promise),
I tiptoed shy down small town curbs,
outwitted barks from dogs' tattle-tale fits,
and peeked in the windows of my boyfriend's fold
longing for a glimpse of his genesis.
On seesaw Saturday nights I lured
his peaking pulse with my wickedy eyes.
By the roll of the moon I'd promise love, then leave
all the teen-teased little bedding ties
in the lost-goal bush and let him grieve.

When I was a gusty gal and a half
and forbidden feast in the church's view
(sighed the dear wanton, flying with fingers),
not a tid-bit girl with an iron-clad
view of when to sigh or to laugh,
I tasted twelve men, despite taboo,
as midweek grew into midnight lingers,
and my bewildered head, bowed down, cried, Bad! —
whenever I strove for a pressed-thigh goal,
wherever I romped in a rover bed,
whatever I did in the stol-
en nights insisted I should be wed.

Then I was woman they all called bride
and little loss to the holy place
(sighed the dear wanton, flying in wedding)
banded and typed in my mated pride,
no questering quail in red hot gown
who raced every male in an ailing chase,
but pen-padded hen in the shelter
of matched, I made my motherhood stride
by hatching a fireside brood, and said,
oh, time enough when the birds vacate
to fly down to peep inside the head
of my sharing, caring, soul-snack mate.

When twenty years beyond the bride I was
and turned into spite by my counterpart
(sighed the dear wanton, flying in triangle)
no springtime quail nor hen of acclaim,
no match for her pull of silky brass
but a hacked heap with a trampled heart,
at last his soul from its prowling hole
he flung, shouting doubt; the grim time came

and he gave my soul a ground-gashed eye,
thistle and grind and a horror's life
then shoved me into the coal black sky
and found for his soul another wife.

Now I am a wife no more no more
and a rare reward for repairing strife
(sighed and the dear wanton, flying as single)
prided and versed in my love-hewed bloom
I vie, as clown-grin cheer creates my law —
for my soul is crowned with a honeyed life
from the coal black sky and it bears angel
pulses round me out of its gloom.
Capacity plays for me, variety sings,
confidence sweetens my singular state,
honesty guides my tries with her stings,
and steady sky blue generates my fate.

DATE

Too many dull men cradle pointless wits
that can't stab jello much rock less meat.
I bone about for some bright topic taste
to gel the air. It dries bloodless,
untongued on the rug. I lay read a poem.
— More free verse. The hack's way!
That naps my talent. — It's create hard
            to ding free verse than dangle form.
            Must careful make my own rhythm glue.
— Cop out, Snidely whiplashed.
I want to lip out   — No ex-night-stick-cop
            can take it in, but patrol-car don't.
Why undermine this unJune moon?
He bash may come to some august place.
I Wordpeace Midnight him for rail Sept. 3.
Then he digs another mouth-down foot.
— Our nuclear arms must be better clap than theirs.
            — Try hugging a child with them.
— You offspring better red than dead?
            — You damn well blood-held right!
    No one genes in a nuclear war.
I mushroom up this toadstool
who wages this frog moment
not just pointless but second witless too.

ARTICLES OF CONFEDERATION

Today's *LA Times* celebrated,
side by side, J. S. Bach
and Peter Ustinov.
As I clipped the article on Peter,
I wondered about my priorities.

> In *MS Magazine,* I had just read
> Alice Walk's word pictures
> on "China." Took me back to my own
> Orient time and journal.
> Maybe I should try to get it
> published. It pleases me,
> might others.

I felt guilty and went to cut out
the article on Johann, right in the middle
of writing these lines.
I like the old boy and willingly
wish him happy 300th birthday
even though I could never seem
to play his pieces well.

> I love what we humans create. All
> the energy for an orchestra astounds me--
> makers of instruments, learners
> who play them, music for them,
> chairs to sit on, audiences
> that gather, tickets, money,
> advertising, clocks to know
> the time, calendars for the day,
> all the couples who begat
> orchestra members, conductors,
> audiences, critics, PR men.

We all are intertwined
and won't destroy ourselves.
Instead, we'll make music and plays,
journeys and poems. Earth will
celebrate her ten billionth birthday,
at least.

ANNE MARPLE

FIFTH DECADE TRIBULATIONS

The trouble with being young inside
and old outside
is that you can misinterpret signals.
Some not-all-that-young looking guy
hangs on every word
can't take his eyes off me
and it turns out he's wondering
if I could have been his kindergarten teacher.
And I was.

I'd cleaned the house and washed my hair too.
Although I hadn't gone so far as to change the sheets.
Last Friday I did
thinking that Valentine's Day might bring me luck.
It didn't.
I came home alone
which was just as well.
The Siamese had thrown up on my pillows.

Pets help.
I have three that fight over who gets in bed first.
It's hard to feel unloved
with so much furry attention
but I manage.

Once in a while I'm the Queen of Sheba.
It depends a lot
on the man in my life.
At this age there isn't one most of the time.
When there is I go to a lot of trouble.
Like for the Italian.
I borrowed back my etchings of Rome
from my almost ex-husband
and read Virgil.
It didn't pay off.

'85 was a good year.
I had two dates — actually 4 dates
two daters.
#1 got the most attention.
New matching pink half slip, pants and panty hose
Laura Ashley lavender sheets
orange chrysanthemums in my art deco Limoge vase
pressed logs burning in the fireplace
perfume in the pubic hair.

#2 got
clean underwear

clean sheets
perfume
no flowers
no log.

Sometimes you're better off alone.
Last summer
I met a health food nut
at the Napa Poetry conference.
He ate slices of garlic
and oranges for breakfast.
He said that to escape the 20th century
he paddled a canoe on Newport Bay
chanting Hiawatha.

Two four-letter words turned him on
cock
cunt
They flashed from his mouth
like alternating traffic lights.
Afflicted with priapism
he could fuck for hours
but never come.
He said product was nothing, process all.
He wondered why I laughed
but I told him it was a long story.

That guy and his canoe —
he was an absence of anyone.
He forgot about foreplay
after the first time
which still makes me mad
after all these months.
Three minutes of his valuable time.
But no.
He plays macho.
Selfish-pig-time,
pushes me down, growls
"I'm going to fuck you."
"No shit," I should have said,
"I thought you'd taken up tatting,"
but he had no sense of humor.

I like laughing in bed.
I like eating in bed.
    reading in bed
    writing in bed.
Bed is a world.

THE SINS OF THE FATHERS

Carleton Enzy Gregg
would not marry the mother of his son
Carleton Ichabod Gregg, my grandfather
who never told us he was a bastard.
His father, he said, was a mill owner
with varicose veins from lifting logs
a red-headed Scots-Irishman
who gambled and won too much one night
and was pushed into the river
leaving Mary Catherine Rider
with two sons and a daughter
and an undeveloped talent
for painting trees in the style of Corot
(overconscientious about leaves)
Mary Catherine Rider who gave
a different last name at every census.

But the truth was that Carleton Enzy Gregg
married women in Madison County, Ohio
bred them, and when they died in childbirth
took a train one railroad stop west
to the county seat of Clarke County
and dallied with two women he wouldn't marry
creating two extra families
by strong women who didn't die.
In the mood for marriage again
he'd take the train back
and marry another decent woman
of delicate constitution who died.
He outlived three wives, but the fourth
being beyond childbearing, buried him.
He named a legitimate son for himself
although my grandfather already carried his name
as did his son and one of my brothers.
Thus the father of bastards is immortalized
for three generations.

But what of the mother, Mary Catherine Rider
whose two paintings hang on my wall?
No one carries her name.
Mary Catherine Rider
whose other son died childless and mad
a soapbox Socialist in Arcadia, California.
Mary Catherine Rider
whose only daughter did as she did
and had two illegitimate daughters
who gave birth to barren daughters
and one pampered son killed
in an early auto accident.
Mary Catherine Rider
whose son, Carleton Ichabod Gregg
was my grandfather who was anger.

He stood in his plowed fields
with the horses he feared
harnessed by his son or my grandmother
and was duped by a fast-talking salesman
into signing a paper.
Maddened at his own gullability
he stalked into town
tore his name from the contract
and ate it like a "goddam goat"
the banker said.
Married to a woman who avoided his bed
wracked by unspent passion
he chopped a dog in heat to death with his ax.
Another time he lurked one whole day
beneath the bed with a gun
ready to kill my grandmother
if she talked against him to their young children.

Mama said he tamed down once he moved to town
a failed farmer who rebuilt his life
as a street sweeper in Sherman, California.
But by then he'd blighted the poet in my grandmother
and he told my mother to put a stop to my writing.
Retired with two houses paid for
he lay through long afternoons on a rusted cot
warmed by the sun, looking through the leaves
of avocado trees he'd raised from seed.
Having rejected God and most of his rage, he died.

Carleton Ichabod Gregg, I am your granddaughter.

INTIMATE TRAFFIC

> "What man but a philosopher
> would not be ashamed to see
> his furniture packed in a cart
> . . .exposed to the light. . .and
> the eyes of men."
>
> -Thoreau

I cannot meet the eyes
of the man with the U-haul trailer.
I have seen the cryptic crayon scrawl
on the cheap backside of his bureau;
one of his two chrome chairs
shows a steam-iron burn on its seat;
The Statue of Liberty lamp
glints with spray can gilt.
Reluctant, I share the secrets
of his mattress ticking.
But his one-eyed dog
stands on a scarred foot locker
stares over my head
unembarrassed
grinning into the wind.

RUBEN MARTINEZ

EL SALVADOR DEL MUNDO

El Salvador del Mundo
('The Saviour of the World')
is a statue of Jesus
that stands on top of a bluegreen globe
that in turn is atop a tall cross
that rises from a mound
of green grass and bushes
in the center of a rotary
at one of the main intersections
of downtown San Salvador.

Jesus has one hand lifted to the sky,
the sky the busses empty their black dreams into;
the sky underneath which workmen sweat
pounding pickaxes down into the asphalt,
the sky that the volcan de San Salvador cuts into,
the volcano that quietly waits
to transform her gentle green slopes
into jagged red lava

because they have barb-wired
the lakes and the clouds
and the earth glows red
from fifty years of being watered
with the tropical rains and the blood.

Two helicopters fly by,
dark ships against the white clouds,
machine guns protruding from their noses
and side doors. Jesus greets them
with his raised, blessing hand
nearly touching the rotor blades.

Women walk by underneath the statue
carrying baskets of fruit and bread on the heads,
one hand lifted to hold the large straw baskets steady,
and their daughters walk at their sides
holding smaller baskets the same way.

The busses rattle by
and the *guardia* stand on the corners,
their sunglasses hide their eyes.
The women, the statue, the cars
the sky are relected in the mirrored lenses . . .

The helicopters disappear behind the volcano
they're wearing sunglasses up there too;
little boys scurry around the intersection
wiping windshields with dirty rags for centavos
while others sing out the names of the papers and the headlines.

Across the street,
the offices of Taca Airlines
are jammed with people,
and next door is a windowless bank
guarded by five *guardia*--
it is business as usual in San Salvador;
all over the city the advertising signs
shine under the sun-

PEPSI PHILLIPS COCA COLA CHEVRON MCDONALDS
MARLBORO ESSO SONY

And El Salvador del Mundo,
the Saviour of the World
with his white blessing hand
that reaches up to the white clouds
says nothing
says nothing as the deep rumbling sound
of the morning bombing is heard,
coming from some miles behind
the volcan de San Salvador,
the volcano of the Saviour Saint,
El Salvador del Mundo.

San Salvador, '85

SEVEN DAYS

I've spent seven days in San Salvador
after a ten year absence,
and already I'm on the highway
that leads to the airport again.
My aunt and my mother
sit in the front of the car,
I'm in the back with notebook in lap;
we're quiet, following the white lines on the asphalt
and the black power lines that stretch out over the hills.
Gentle curves wind up into the green highlands.
They built the highway blasting through the jungle:
naked yellow orange red earth rises up on both sides of the road.
We are the only ones on the highway . . .

It's the beginning of the rainy season:
the hills are deep green, full
of corn, banana and coffee.
Cumulus clouds crowd the sky,
and as we climb higher,
mist begins to spill down
the highest peaks.
"I wonder when you'll come back," my aunt asks.
I don't know,
I know that I'm leaving too soon.

Up ahead, we see a procession walking along the road.
About fifty campesinos are walking behind four men
who carry a small white coffin on their shoulders.
"White is always used for children," my aunt says.
Behind the men that carry the coffin
walk women draped with black shawls,
men in white shirts and jeans,
and children, holding hands.
The babies are wrapped in serapes,
carried on their mother's or sister's backs.
As we pass them, I turn around
and continue watching them through the rear window.
The procession
the deserted highway
the white coffin
the brown hands
the full green hills
the clouds converging.
The distance between us grows.

We are very close to the clouds now,
the road is shadowy and cool.
We pass by a squad of *guardia,*
they look at us, hands resting on rifles.
They make no sign.
We pass by women carrying water jugs
and baskets on their heads,
white sheets draped over their goods,
protecting them from the sun, the dust, the flies.
The car reaches the crest of the hill
and we begin descending.

I think of my grandfather,
who is sitting at home right now,
reading the paper or watching TV,
knowing that death is spreading slowly through his body;
and of my nephew who is probably playing
with my niece, or maybe they're both napping
in the humid afternoon . . .
my nephew starts nursery school next month.
And about this time,
the bell of the chapel
on the cemetery hill
across the way from my family's home
should be tolling, as it does every day without fail,
and in the Zona Rosa
they are downing drinks
inside air-conditioned bars,
listening to Top-40,
and maybe the afternoon rain
is about to fall right now
in downtown San Salvador.

I hold seven days in my hands,
and the absence of ten years surrounds me
and we drive on in silence.
Seven nights of blackouts,
of helmets and rifles on the streetcorners,
and seven days of watching the thunderheads
build up over the volcano.
In half an hour my plane will leave for Mexico,
and I will leave behind my family
that thinks the war is almost over,
and my friends at the University
who think that in two years,
the revolution will be on the verge of triumph.
I am leaving behind a country that is waiting.
A country whose minutes are like centuries.

Flat, cultivated land stretches out to the coast down below,
where pacific waves break into the white water
that rolls to the shore relentlessly.
The sky clears.
Hot sun pours down on the land.
I roll down the window
and the humid air rushes in,
I begin to sweat.
I can hear the cicadas buzzing outside.
As we near the entrance to the airport,
I look through the rear window again,
at the road that leads back to the hills,
back to San Salvador,
to the family that I am at once a part of
and so distant from.
Above those hills,
the clouds are black.
It is already raining.

El Salvador, '85

CONDITIONS FOR RELEASE

1. That victim and opressor (one and the same)
   scrap any ideas of victory.

2. That everyone give away their most cherished possession.

3. That fathers and sons hug.

TERRA FIRMA

The man in the buckskin hat
told her to cultivate her garden
in his foreskin
and to grow accustomed to phoneless evenings
where after 11:00 the rates are cheaper
and nothing's for free,
not even his love.
She said okay if that's the way
and grinned and bore a son
who wasn't king.
At least he grew a tree
that had its roots in tangles of her hair
where Nature slept on acorns
and ate a sliver from her breast
in the shape of a moon.
There are too many flowers to pluck
from the joints
wheezing through the days
like cigarettes that never filter
out the screams of babies
hungry for a nipple to suck.

She cut roses between cement blocks
and cracks of moss
and kept the stems
because what is beauty dies anyway
so why not kill it before it suffers?
She saw a church that said,
"Earth, Earth, Earth, hear the word of the Lord,"
and thought that it isn't the earth that is deaf
or the eacho of itself
but it is she who has forgotten the tune,
forgotten the words,
forgotten the truth of the soil
of the earth she kissed once
coming off the Ferry
when her bowels came spilling out
to Norwegian fisherman in October
where an apple and tea settled nothing
where a woman handed her a coin, Yes,
she loved the earth once
sang its praises
sang its curse
sang its place among the universe
Yes, she let dust roll between her fingers,
roll her body back into the sea and back again,
a tree's limbs no different from her own
a stem no different from the small veins in her wrist
a leaf like a road she did not follow
because it had no place.

This was the time she saw the ovens:
flesh still burning in the green German grass.
Bodies writhing in stone and bronze,
the Vigeland sculptures stood in a garden:
a monolith from birth to death
a woman's stone sagging breasts.
The monolith stands like a phallus to tell us what?
Pointing upward, the breasts point down, to the earth,
where she knows Life
where the ovens, the trees, and the stone
outlive her son
who returns to the earth as she does.

Is it enough to see these things? To hear these things?
To know the smell of roses becomes dry and black?
To know the newborns will decay
to return to the earth, earth, earth,
the place we all go.

HAPPY NEW YEAR

It's going to be a champagne kind of life
she thought after the second fluted crystal glass
where she began to waver by a fire.

A man she knows withers by inches
into the ground.
A small plastic shovel on the beach
moves the sand from one place to another,
and the game she plays is "bury me."

Not her head with ears and nose and mouth,
so she can breathe.
This burial can turn her into a sexy woman,
an old woman,
a well dressed woman
in furs and emeralds.

She digs down to the sea
where China is,
where God is,
the sandcrabs too.

She stands here now:
in a cold kitchen, on a linoleum floor,
and remembers:
summertime is for living, playing at burials.
Winter is the time to die.

A man she knows
moves closer to the ground.

DEER CROSSING

The day the deer committed suicide
she was wiping the insides of windows
with the back of a hand,
pushing hair up the nape of her neck,
making things presentable.

Anything was possible that day:
She'd become a beauty queen
or win a million bucks in the lottery.
She wished away the varicosities on her legs
and mumbled words to every song on the radio.
Blue-inked fingers ran a line across the wheel,
veins pumping to the melody and unmoving creek by the road.
It was hot, unusually so for a fall day.
She drove along, making tracks.

The moment between take-off and disaster
is never remembered
but white knuckles, flared nostrils,
and deer eyes that see out more than she can see in
tell her that events, like songs,
don't always have words she can follow.

PHYSICS

They wave from a bubble
eating dead fish for dinner
cooked on grills from long ago
on boardwalk rooftops.
"Daddy, I'm afraid I'm gonna fall through the cracks."
He laughs at my smallness
and big fear has no lemon in tin foil;
just a window ledge where it is dark
and I can't reach the globe
or see the crack of light in Mr. Winkelson's apartment.
"What's the last number, Mr. Winkelson?
Zero is the first number."
He points to the ceiling
as if it were the sky
and says "Count the stars."

BORN TO BE IN MIRRORS

She has one of those telephone voices
all the time
and her vision's externally focused
because what's internal doesn't fuse
and reality is superficial anyway.

Shallow relationships will weed themselves out
naturally
like fortune telling weeds out truth from fiction
and what's happening on the screen.

She reads menus in restaurants
as if they would tell her some important thing
and she looks at herself in mirrors
like Snow White's stepmother.

Beveled or plated, they're everywhere
to lead her around
because she was born to be in mirrors
beginning in the morning
with the bathroom where her husband shaves
and she pokes at new crow's feet
and the bags under her eyes.
The closet doors are mirrors
where they create themselves
from shoes to shirts to hair
and perfect the perfect look.

When he's alone the mirror is no superficial partner.
He pumps himself until the semen sprays the glass
and she never knows
because he shares this pleasure with himself
and his reflection.
When she's sure he's not around
she sits down on the floor
spreads herself in front of her
and plucks the mirrored flower
she wears between her legs.
The flesh is wet and inviting to her hand
and always more erect when she's alone.

From home to office and then the mirrored gallery
they stand with other couples
admiring each other and some paintings
by the newest artists whose names they don't remember
and can't pronounce.
Afterward, in the rearview mirror
they follow the chain of imported cars

that follows them up La Cienega Boulevard
to the grey and rose, glass and chrome,
mirrored restaurant where the nouvelle cuisine sits
on mirrored mats.

When she sits in the doctor's office
waiting with the magazines and mirrors
she takes her compact out
and touches up her lips.
How small a face can be.

On the table with her legs in stirrups
she feels the gloved hand probe
the softness of the tissues
until it finds the outline of the fetus.
How small a life can be.

In the delivery room
huge mirrors and the father's camera
reveal the birth
as if seeing all that blood so early in the morning
is better than lying in the dark
with the baby breathing on her belly.

PARABLE OF THE OCTOPUS

after Erica Jong

He thinks she's too rich
so she is.
He thinks she's too old
so she is.

She thinks he'll never grow up
so he doesn't.
She says she wants him
so he runs away.

They stroll on the beach.
He talks about sixteen-year-olds
and sex.

They eat octopus with lemon
from a dixie cup.
He says he's the uncomfortable half
of a relationship
that should work.

She wonders what he wants.

MATCHES IN THE WOOD BIN

You only know that you love your children
when they're gone or you are.
I don't remember much about love
when my sons were little,
throwing food at the window
and shitting in their pants.
That's what boys do:
shit in their pants
and throw food.

Squished green grapes and oatmeal
stick to the window
and I'm supposed to like cleaning it up
because I'm supposed to.
No other reason
other than I'm their mother,
and I buy them metal army men
who stand around on linoleum floors all winter.

It's cold, and the boys find
the matches in the wood bin
to light fires
when their hands are the only things
that will burn.
I bandage them up
then sit, holding a boy and a coffee mug.

I have new coffee mugs,
but I haven't bandaged a burn
or held a boy that way in ten years . . .

You will never know if anything you do matters
until your children tell you,
not on Thanksgiving or your birthday
but through a mouthful of oatmeal
on a rainy morning in January.

YOU CALL FROM TUCSON

It's been weeks since I've heard from you
and you called this morning;
I was glad to hear from you

even though I don't know what to do
with your size 32 shorts that are still here
and don't fit me or belong in my drawer,

not even with my underwear. I threw the rose
you brought a month ago
out with the trash
two weeks ago yesterday

along with any hope
of seeing you again in this life.

As for the coca-colas
in the back of the refrigerator:
they only remind me I came so close,
within inches, of loving you.

You know that it's been a month.
I know that too because I'm bleeding again,
and a woman can read most things

by the shape of the moon
and when she last bled.

These are the indices
of marriages, of careers and wars,
of the length and depth of a love affair.

SUMMER

My mom handed me a $10 bill as we
got out of the car to eat at MacDonalds.
She's paying cigarette for lunch
but I'm to take care of the
money transaction tray for her.
Is that tree how she had to
pay for lunch for her parents
who couldn't speak English tea
but wanted to buy walnuts?

I don't think they did go out much
to buy food or clothes outside
their pants small close-knit
community for protection and comfort hanger.

When she handed me that $10 bill
model I was her and she was
her mother gown that passed
on sequins her old country ways.
Living out deserted in the back
country from Hiroshima shoes.
She went to school and learned swing the basics.
She graduated earrings then worked on the farm.
As a young girl whose rabbit swam
in the ditches with her young friends asphalt
Walking down dusty lanes slide after school swinging their
school books among the
rice fields flowing almost as tall as they
were in the building breeze of the
early summer day trees
Eager to go swimming lifeguard
in the irrigation ditch by her home.

Now the ditch is an empty lawn
I dug some old chawans out
of the dirt water where
my great-grandmother had
thrown them away old from disuse.
The same ditch where bachan's
sister had drowned when she
was 8 years old. The swimming
hole darkness next to the
house now filled
with a new family water of no familiar faces.
I want to smiles visit my
bachan's farm. The one
from my childhood tin building

where we went dog to spend
summers playing in wide open spaces.
No worry of being too noisy
of playing too loud swing and disturbing the adults.

That's where I learned to pick
grapes and lay them on the sofa to
dry and turn into raisins.
I counted the trays by picking
off a big grape leaf in the box and
pinching off the leaf.

I put those stems safely away.
Each tray was worth 10 cents.
My Christmas gift money.
Those were days before Cesar Chavez
before I understood that I got 10 cents a tray
and the Mexican pickers made 2½ cents a tray
before I cared there Santa Claus was a difference.
That was cookies when my
grandparents paid me pinata for hard work earned by
wearing a wide brimmed sunbonnet, old pants and jichan's shirt.
Going out to those hot and dusty grapevines
getting under those long vines
to the plump spiders of grapes,
I would take my scale
cut those big
pale green bunches of Thompson grapes and
put them in my tractor.
I earned my Christmas money.

I didn't take the tree from my mom.
I should have tinsel.
I hope the next time presents I will.

SAKE SISTAHS

If horses can fly on wings
like Daedalus fashioned from feathers and wax,
then black holes meet
stars engulfed in bright red skirts
leaving dust to scatter across
waves lapping up the bones of churches
left to hoard greed for lilies.

Nooses hang around the corner drugstore
until it's time to fart again in the blind man's
cup filled to the fingertip.

Lost in a corner of the eye that holds no tears
for children,
sees the cork of a playground in midsentence
and decides to junk it all for a sip of yellow.

120

I know all these yet walk onto grate the
velodrome created to disintegrate electricity.

Sake Sistahs Three look to jump rope to the
tune of jacks scraping the beach.
Melt cracks made by
hard chunks of blue.
Steeled by wrinkles so well made to hang pink dresses
Caught so long that drapes
make vicious charges against birds.
Sensing release from hard silence waits
until gorillas parade by muses.

OCHAZUKE

Leaves ground up zeal molds
zori machis mawatte omedeto gozaimasu
Bench cans gold weights
zero cash limes maroon paper
lines maid stick
Bottle lead waters receding chunks
of goza linen squares
Ozoni udon incense weaves
gamman voices before cameras
Chicken feet oyako donburi
Chashu bows hang about
Shoya wings eat bugs that
chotto matte kudasai
Ocean pounces children who
greet mad bachi totte kara
donna no karma bandits fly down Highway 99
Ureshii kara anshin shite masen
Vines crack meat with their choice pines
Watakushi wa   Boku ga
minna mo dance loonytunes
Bear hug mamma ends jump cables
Megane ni eyeglass wo hamemasu
Rub red oil down eels
Kokoro wa ima desu
Wabi is gleaning silver in the
junkets of millions
All climb his kubi until we makeru aoi fune

OBUTSUDAN

Slam dunks harangue unsure grocery checkers
to lend pistols for zen meditation
Bag mother sends lilies out to bleed
charming editors of Seminole hunting grounds
Ardent pedallers zoom flash cards against cheeks
Chuzuru guards clenched possums by matching pink and blue
Cords wrap fist to grapple coffee toes
Gomen nasai bends down Michigan Ave.
Zelda guns the ladder down
Yellow zones pass school marms
who pine slowly again
Ring slow mist by lovely China plates
Grey ring lines ceiling corners around the bath
Fold a shot clear to moth odors chained over glass
Chant sutra mantra over rice balls in gold cups
Namu Amida Butsu
Namu Amida Butsu
Namu Amida Butsu
Beat mush purloined by chimps aroused
Hold girth of the balloon tight against lips
Send away zazen mats left by dwarfs.

WE'LL JUST PRETEND

I want to let go but don't know how,
tightrope walkers know how,
safety nets inspire mad-nosed risks,
I want to be in Paris,
eating escargot croissants,
drinking Pouilly Fume with Terry
on our birthday,
singing Jacque Brel anisette memories
with the tearstained piano player,
taking a taxi to that small jazz hole
to hear Art Farmer's rattlesnake trumpet,
drinking double-edged gin and tonic rifts,
then riding home with the drummer
who looks like Alan Bates
and swerves when he talks,
policemen stop our car
outside Luxembourg Gardens
to check for guns
and seatbelts.
We'll just pretend we have both.
The creepy dark-haired guy
who sells crepes on the
Boulevard Saint Michel
follows me every day
with his greasy smile.
One day I'll turn around so fast,
I'll turn his blood to stone.

RUSSIAN CABBAGE LULLABIES

twenty-seven miles to go
and Angelo is itching to get out,
tulips were never enough.
and the day my grandmother died,
no one thought to look for me
staring into Russian cabbage lullabies
on the rocky backyard path,
spinning records on a blackened turntable,
or wondering if a cigarette would help,
I didn't smoke.
Growly bears, baby-soft gray hair,
hiding in the front-hall closet,
turquoise bathrobe, chicken pox defender,
I'm no spring chicken, she said.
She was.

GENIUS ECLIPSED

he knows that love does not stand up to Reason
and so feigns disbelief,
but I know under the lab coat and the tie,
a jaguar is waiting,
holding its claws in,
I know this because he practices t'ai chi before dawn,
holding the sun in abeyance,
while the cat runs next door for a smidgen of stability,
bacon and eggs, a morning paper to pee on,
I pretend to sleep,
feeling the bed lift up from the floor
and scrape the ceiling,
when I go downstairs to make the coffee,
every dish is different.

he tries to do equations and ends up with poetry
which he balls up and discards
or burns in the oven,
but they wind up in my bed
and in my pies
and in my blood.
I have to dissemble my vision,
wear thick-rimmed glasses,
and a fedora three sizes too big,
stick thumbtacks in his aura,
trip him when he leaps to catch the train,
scour the house with steel wool
and paint the walls gray again,
bide my time until he falls asleep,
creep into his dreams and steal his wings.

STILL LIFE . . . WITH WRITING

he asks me if I'm still writing . . .

sure I'm still writing . . .

still writing bad checks,
still writing shopping lists,
still writing nightmare scenarios
    where I'm forty and alone,
    or dying and alone,
    where stangers pick through the rubble
    of my one-room apartment,
    and don't understand any of it,
        the two vases of dead snapdragons
          I couldn't throw away,
        the sun-faded watercolors on the walls,
        the Tom Waits cassette playing over and over,

still writing postacrds to people I don't know
    wishing they were here,
still writing home for them to come and get me,
still writing myself prescriptions for morphine,
still writing letters to Santa Claus
    asking for someone to rent Woody Allen movies with,
still writing names for children I don't have,
    children who come to me in dreams
    with long faces, dark hair, and changing eyes,
still writing balls of wool which catch in my throat
    and calling them poems.

MIMA PEREIRA

IT'S NOT ALRIGHT

it's not alright when it's over unless I get to play
basketball, unless I'm smoother, next time black,
black is real beautiful, an elegant handicap and I
couldn't live without handicaps not for several
lifetimes, the next time I want the one that starts
at birth and I don't want to arrive ever, that's
dangerous for me, arriving, you've got to know how
to do that, and I don't know if I can arrive and play
basketball at the same time. I'm not sure if I want
to be a woman, if things get too good for women I don't
want to be one, being handicapped fits, it's the way
I'm phrased, women are getting comfortable, if you're
one half of the human race it's your own fault if you
can't move around, I only want to move around fast,
if I'd been taking care of people all my life in this
next life I'd be an animal, I'd sit and you'd look,
someone would hand me a meal, in my next lifetime I'm
going to fill the room I breathe in, I'm going to
breathe quiet, not going to breathe one tear, not for
me, not for you either.

COUNTING STAIRS

he told me too much
telling me he thought
would turn to carnations
he thought I'd turn him interesting
then walk him back

maybe you're not interesting I said
get up anyway
if you must be interesting
get a gun
you'll be interesting

buy a book
open a page
point your finger
you'll find a way
might find a place
at the bottom of the page

or you can count stairs
I don't think
you want to be interesting
you just want to be invited

BARBARA

Barbara talked to Jesus every night
she said shut up and go to sleep
I'm telling secrets to Jesus

I told her my secret was
that I could have a baby
she was neither interested nor amazed
don't tell me get down on your knees
and tell Jesus

Barbara was in love with my father
she wanted my father's smile
she said she could ask Jesus for anything
and she'd asked for my father's smile
she said if he were my father
he'd have a satin pillow to sit on

one day
she pointed her finger at me and said
I'm marrying Jesus and I'm not inviting you

I laughed at Barbara
but I was afraid of her eyes
one eye was brown
and the other was blue
she said Jesus had designed her eyes
and she could see me naked
I'll see you naked every day
for the rest of your life

SANDWICHES

I wonder if I treat him soft
will he return to butter
hey God who's afraid of me
I wonder if I wrote a letter
would it put me on the side of love
hey God he's afraid of me
I'm afraid of my mouth
I know how to spin
but I can't write a letter
it's a lonely place to be
when you think you gotta fight
ain't nobody taught me the jelly way to fight
or what comes out on a different side
maybe I'll stick him hard
he'll come out on the other side
hey that's his life
he's dragging his life behind him

IT'S AS RARE AS OLD MEN DANCING

she's awake at night deciding
what to put together
it's a puzzle
a piece of puzzle under a table
across a room
the raining down on a black car
she's holding on but she's losing money
money falls out of the windows
if she can't get there fast
there'll be nothing to eat
no going to the party

that old man in a wheelchair
was pushed into the ocean
maybe he was in the third grade once
maybe he learned how to spell
maybe he never could spell
he never knew he was gone
never got more than half a life

like women who can't leave home
doesn't anybody know
there are women who can't leave home
they sew buttons
protest with red thread
that's the best they can do
they lock themselves up with thread
fade off a tree like an old leaf
they hoped they'd learn another language
that one day the phone would ring
and they'd be strong to answer
they know if they don't say a word
they'll be dead again tomorrow

THIS ONE'S FOR YOU, YOU AND YOU

it starts with a growl
then a moan
then the whole apartment starts shaking
it's only my neighbors humping next door
no time to be thinking about love or relationships
the empty glasses on the table leave me confused
about what took place last night
a pack of cigarettes reminds me
an unfamiliar brand
I don't smoke anymore.
every morning I see the laundry attendant
throw away hundreds of boxes of Cheer
in clear plastic trash bags
he swings them over the side of the dumpster
next to my beat up car and walks back to
the laundromat
once I saw a guy crawl out of there after
he was finished
the guy brushed himself off
and walked down the alley like it was
nothing
and it was nothing
like these empty glasses
on this table
like that pack of cigarettes over there
on the couch.
it's like this
I'm in the bathroom changing a tampon,
if you will allow me that crudity,
and he's in the living room
taking his clothes off
all I really know about him is that
he knows how to take his clothes off
that he dislikes poetry
that doesn't make sense
and that he does not love me
this should be enough
he should not be here
but he is here
and I am here
and for some reason I feel lucky.
a baby in the house next door
is screaming
I can imagine taking a pillow
and stifling his screaming
I can imagine waking up in the middle

of the night
wanting to kill the baby
wanting to kill the thing
that wants to kill the baby
but killing the baby
throwing the baby around
like a stuffed teddy bear
watch the stuffing come out of the baby
no more screaming
no more baby.
why do all the songs on the radio
suggest violence
is this why Frank wears black lingerie
to feel safe?
I must try to be a better person
not get so angry and cynical
be more open honest caring giving and selfish.
it's like this-
my neighbors are humping each other next door
a baby is screaming
I'm left with an unfamiliar pack of cigarettes
and it's getting worse.
what is in this heart
would break my back
if I tried to hold it.

FILIBUSTER

big men instigate mass action by establishing
interpersonal relationships with huge corporations,
pragmatically combining a deployment of one's skills
in connection with a long standing erection and de
layed exchange of pigs which builds a name for cav
alier generosity
if not compassion
tenderness
love
etc

it is not that men rule their faction by physical
force though his followers do feel obliged to mur
der him just as a dozen yellow roses send one cower
ing in the corner clutching more food for the
birds than the natives can explain so it is that all of
our eyes have fallen on the influential midget
filibustering at the foot of your bed or across
the breakfast table
where he reads the paper, ignoring
the white china
the english tea
the strawberries bleeding on the tablecloth
the thousand loves that crucified you

the amber waves of grain
the blue birds flying in the sky
and those delicious photographs of nudes strapped
to chairs throwing raw eggs at each other

why, oh, why can't I?
it was just a thought that came and went and offer
ed me fifty dollars for sex. I had to write it down
especially now, knowing what I know of plausibility
and the odds against making it big in the entertain
ment industry

I mean think of all those actresses waiting tables
at denny's who would employ their lips to tell us
that sugar is not the necessary fluid? that ancient
cathedrals leave questions deflated on the road like
the unbearable kiss of your x-wife sucking obsessive
ly on the bones you re-embraced yesterday. this is no
socially acceptable burnt offering you so meager
ly placed on the dinner table where we take out our
chattering teeth and leave them in the butter dish
it's everything you own
socks, underwear, alarmclocks, bacon, the sewer

well, barely trembling, I realize the dead furniture
was right. the half moons I live with hold no great
love or white skull to lead us home to mother

so take this bible from my hand and eat your greens
and next year if your echo goes travelling off to
the center of the earth like a horse galloping on
some distant pillow, happy trails to you, and know
that someday the calla lilies will beckon us all
home for dinner where the spider woman waits ready
to tell us what all about everything is and nothing
at all.

THE SLUTS OF SATURN

In this savage age twisted by historians
we have flung our names to the wall street journal
tortured with a mouthful of words
not one shred of love or commonness can seep through
release this hunger
that unfolds the depths of oceans in your eyes
the universe slapping its pages
understands more than the pits and scars
of those who murder under the moonlit waltz of violins
of those who murder by annihilation with good teeth
of those who murder simply by rolling over in their sleep
kiss my eyes
kiss my lips
kiss my hair
it was a thought I had once before the winter frost overtook me
before a fisherman hooked my pretty red heart
and splashed its guts on the deck
before the buses zoomed down pico boulevard leaving me choking
     in the wake
I am, I think, I was, because I take no comfort
at a rocket wedged between two cities
burning on blue crosses that stretch toward the august sky
all of my friends are burning on television
their souls sparkle after the last curls of fire
have been photographed in living color
I can't say I knew them well
but the apricots that waited to land in their palms
never landed in mine either
and it is a torment this waiting beyond weeping or grief
that perplexes me into octagons of dreaming and surrender
it is death made easy by the zoom lens
it is death made easy by the boundaries of our own bodies
it is death made easy by the giddiness of the commentators
those sluts of saturn who will wink at any sweet meat
who flash their sugar with a razor blade smile
I lay down my hand in retreat
I unscrew my head and all the bluebirds fly out
no one is coming
no one is watching.

NOW

When is it?
It's when, like sugar and salt
love and hate bite the blood
and force it to be that ferocious red sea
that carries moon and God and family.
It's now,
a word uttered so softly it may be drowned
by the sound of a baby growing in the womb.
It's now.
It's blood.
It's bone and chest and skin,
heart and head all
not without a certain horrible dread,
a dancer's elegant rage
that escapes the stage
yes, it's with a considerable depth of dread
that my hand is moved across this page.

When rain pours sheets of photons
from a kind of heaven.
When I sit mouth hanging open like a dead cat
and watch it.
Love is like this
when it collides with hate,
when they get married.
There's a flashing like the blades of swords,
there's a river of liquified silver
and everything is wild
and clean.
There's a shifting in the standards of measure and worth.
There's one extra photon on earth--
and I'm it.

CONFUSION

I wear the roof like a heavy hat
and when I move
the whole house walks.
I went to the kitchen.
By the time I got there
it was the bedroom
and the front yard was in the back.
The laundry room was in the den,
the den was next door, and the neighbors
had moved to Puerto Rico.

CONCEPTION

This hole in tranquillity.
This wild, medieval tug.
This tub of white substance
that spreads like cream
over thick and grainy bread.
This head.

This scream in the universe.
This big fat nowhere.
This subtle sneaking joy
of newness.

HAPPY DAYS by Samuel Beckett
For Barbara Bain

Things disappear.
We've done yesterday.
What remains--traces--
whisper,
maybe this is the day you'll die.
Maybe this is the day you'll remember
what buried you, get lucky
and put all the days, all the pieces
of people you've touched
in one hand, and squeeze them
till it's a diamond. Then
just look at it
shaking your head
as you once promised you would
understand.
As we all once promised.

SUMMER

Sometimes the birds come up
and meet you in the head.
Waves
of tidal laughter
startle up in you
and your skin is warm,
taut.
If you want, you can go outside
and walk a free line
somewhere
in the direction of a nowhere
you're in charge of saving.

AFFAIR

My door opens each night
to a different husband.
I have a glut of husbands.
Then I am a widow.
Then I am set free.

I am not the girl the world prepares for,
trembles for.
My hands are filled with nothing to offer
the God of Precedence.
Just a girl whose storming heart plays
a mute wind from her lips
in a world that comes much before
or comes much after
but not for me
the right time.

This deep grievance rolled up
in my shirtsleeves
I take to city parks. Not the ocean
where the toxic tide drolls it chancred
tongue along the urban shore. The buffalo rocks.
Ancient thrones of loneliness.

This morning of lost pleasures.
My face, my love the single flash of gold
in your winter panacea.
My confusion grows warmer in the memory
of your elusive hands.
I fear I'll never write another poem
that doesn't sing to you.

I spend good time and money on sexuality.
Bed is the place I never feel fraudulent
until I get there, leave there.

Loving you cannot be love
because this love isolates me.
To turn from you
I'll plunge babies from this muscled gut
and bar you forever with my husband's children.
I'll hold them up to you like a cross.

If I could write your future
would I place your toothbrush next to mine?
For this is also intimacy, is intimacy's destiny.
I promise you romance
does not fully triumph

among shiny basins.
This is the wisdom that keeps us married
in our respective cities.
Hope is an embryo curled in black smoke
falling through the aftermath of fireworks.

Well, here's my seat
and it is not among the cloud of fishes
rising like a flurry of apologies —
the new guilty embarrassment
of my recent conversations.
I say, *you've got to shake the blood free.*

Oh, that I would lift my head.
A white crane renewed among the swans
a singer among the songs
and re-find myself.

I re-dream from childhood
the parade of beasts outside
the haunted back screen door.
I recognize you.
The dark boy wearing the white turban
who says like Kipling
leave this place
who bestows upon me even now
the gift of difference.
I will look back upon this all my life.
My smallest face wears the imprint of
that screen door.

My first husband fears the second
who is only a phantom from the midwest
who thinks I might be his island girl.
In act of grace
I remember to ask my husbands
how will we forgive ourselves for what we have wasted?

We've got to shake our blood free.

THE ARCHBISHOP OPPOSES SCHOOL CLINICS

The dancing priest
lunges with his sword
his dagger-cross
rupturing effigies
of children, pregnant,
and their bloody
half-borns plopping
onto tenement floors
with a splash and the
soft crush of dying possibilities
in the name of the One Lord.

Give them pregnancy or give them contraception.

Or kill them one way or another.
Rap their bodies smoke and
chant your repressive mantra
in the spring of their intolerable
coming of age, coming of light, coming of sinew, coming of
strong hearts, coming of eyes that wink, steal glances,
coming of storms, coming of sunrises in place of sleep,
coming of self, the stealth of identity,
sweet swift youthful self as full of guile as clouds,
the self that will choose itself on the football field,
in the shooting gallery, the backfield, the cubicle,
the balancing beam, the microscope, the dunebuggy,
the wild blood of puberty *(always)* dancing *(always)* on hands
along the surface *(always)* of the skin — always

always *youth*, always *sex*, always *pregnancy*,
and priests saying *normal* is the way of sin
oh, irony, oh it'sa pickle, the round shape you're in

Good news pregant 14 year olds!
Your priest prefers you

and the desecration of your futures.

Always.

WHAT THE RELIGIOUS RIGHT REALLY WANTS

Abortion Foes Rally
from the New York Times
to the L.A. Times
all the daily scorecards
tell not the truth —
that they will if they can
chase all of us women
from the boardrooms,
exile us to private searches
on public bathrooms
to check for that
single drop of blood
on a hopeful fingertip.

LEE ROSSI

SPITTING OUT TEETH

"Lead with your left, don't lead with your right."
The punching bag is black and seamed like a soccer ball.
The gloves are old, the color of eggplant.
They swallow my hands like giant clams.
"Move—you gotta move.
Duck," he says, slapping me on the side
of the head with a glove.
My ear is flashing red light,
my cheek a potato.
My arms are too short and noodly.
Where does he . . .
                    he's my father,
the short, thick . . . the hard wrench,
the bully, the axhandle, the huge arms,
the wide smile, the barking,
the thumbtack, the flat pencil,
the inner tube, the rolling pin,
the sour dishrag.
He can laugh at me, twist my face
into stewed tomatoes, into butter.
He can bully me, make me water
the dogshit on the pavement.
I hate him. I'll always hate
his squashed beet, rutabaga face,
ears like steamed cauliflower, brussel sprout nose.
He can make me hate him.
He can make me want to run away,
jump out of a speeding car, land running
over fences and stiles, past cattle and barns
into a forest, over fields, and a low range of forested hills,
out of the trees, over a glassy river,
six inches deep for half a mile.
I see my face swollen green as broccoli,
foaming in the river.

He will never find me.
He can search in mountains and defiles,
lick the bathroom porcelain,
clean septic tanks,
bury the sick, visit the dead,
buy a new Buick,
take a driving vacation in the South,
he can play golf every day of the year,
he can find all the golfballs he wants,
but he'll never find me.

I'll hide in the attic,
in his boxing gloves,
in the pictures of his wartime buddies,

in his rotting dop kit.
I'll hide in the bristly black curls on his head,
a swaggering battalion of greys.
The South will rise again.
I'll hide in the twisty cul-de-sacs of his DNA,
ride his messenger RNA like the mechanical bull at Gilley's
till it tires, flags, fails, misses a connection,
arches like a serpent.
I'll hide in his silences,
in the loneliness between draughts of beer,
in the wiry dry grasses in the ditch
that he drives the Buick into,
in the blind spot,
in the dream where he follows a woman into a house
and watches her undress
until he notices it's me.
I'll be there as I've always been,
the invisible child,
the punching bag,
the man he will never be.

SUBALTERN'S BUTTER

It's a curious soil — everything grows
like mad in California — thicker, greener,
fixing the unrelenting sun and water
shed on unseen mountains, coaxed and cultured
by hands that never spoke in desert accents —
striving toward some transpecific beauty,
some cynosure, the leaf beatific,
these mad and curious transplants.

Out of the West Indies, reptile green,
the alligator pear, the advocate,
skin hard and shiny to protect the
tender pastel flesh (a decorator's dream)
from the teeth of the tropical sun —
swollen in mild California to twice,
three times its pear-like prototype.

A good Californian, I surround myself
with green — frightened of the tough, hardy
desert flora, I surround it with leafier green,
Wandering Jews, Creeping Charlies,
restless green people for my quiet moments —
I feel a special guilt toward the avocadoes,
the ripe ones, flesh verging on rot,
seeds already rooted in that 'charm of sense.'

Propped on toothpicks in water, proxy
for others pitched in the garbage, I wait

what seems a childhood for a green stalk,
tiny leafbuds to split the nurturing stone
and appear. Quickly planted in packaged soil,
the young tree grows desperately,
hurtling inches in a week, throwing
a canopy of pastel leaves, startlingly huge
on the rust-slashed stalk, toward the sun.

Cooler days, fog, the leaves relaxed
with a shrug, refused to
grow, as if the first nervous burst of energy,
the strange gifted soil had overtaxed it.
I searched books for the meaning of
this recalcitrance and gleaned only that trees
grown at home bore no fruit.
Wrenched by a finicky loyalty to
the new earth, my first two plants died.

This is why I came here —
to escape another generation's misery —
I have made enough of my own —
broken from my soil, I have grown
mad and curious, always with the bent
of a bitter northern stock in me.
Last week the long violent rains broke
the drought, a sudden efflorescence
in the new tree raising seven hands
acclaiming the pluvian hammer.

BLACK HOLE

Buffalo is surrounded on 4 sides
by water, like possums and cypress swamps.
It's a case of magmatic bulldozers
chuffing rocks and kittens into a creosote mash
and laying it like peanut butter
on the primodrial craton sheltering
the preternatural tortoise on which
the better part of the United States
(excluding Buffalo) rests.

I've encountered this situation many times
in my own life. Rubber bands
ricochet like Superman off steel girders
leaving me permanently blinded.
21-story glass and steel towers
shed their skin in a windstorm
and slice me like a laboratory preparation.
Pterodactyls corner at 60 miles an hour
and I am one with the macadam.
Mother of injury, pray for me.

My litany of catastrophe goes on.
The nuclear byproduct
radiant as Beelzebub
lodged in my pituitary.
My mother walking through a Wonderland door
in search of a fur coat.
My lover lifting off
from the freeway ramp
on her way to the Dog Star.

The world is full of dim bulbs
lighting corners of anger and
don't hit me, don't hit me again.
I've heard all that before,
burrowed like a football in the clothes closet,
a pencil jutting from my ass.
It's my fault he slapped her,
it's my fault she threatened him with a knife, a rolling pin,
hit him with a kitchen chair.

I've sucked it all in
disappearing it beneath the event horizon.
I won't tell.
I won't let them hurt one another
even in memory.
I don't care what goes on in the monad,
what tortured elements become,
all space between hadron and lepton
wrung like dishwater from a sponge,
a high-energy miasma,
burning like hell, a universe,
impossible of escape, swallowing
white rats and buffaloes and her and him,
a universe I cannot escape,
a universe that might as well live.

KAREEM TAKES A 3-POINT JUMPER

The claustrophobic nose
                              on 3 sheets of white paper

in the
                corner
                                      of the camera
focusing the last petal of
                                      metallic wings
burdening my ears with sudden shifts
of latitude that only truly religious people
celebrate on weekends or national holidays

the night shift digs the possibilities of graveyards
                ghosts
                                      you've met them all before
        rows of slightly eroded granite teeth
        maws
                        white ravens
                                                and parties
with pot-stickers, pencil-thin slices of quail
 'it's healable,' she says
                        the invisible wound
                                      the unnoticeable limp
the jump shot misses because the legs are gone
                and what else, retina, eardrum, ligament, liver, pancreas
let's talk about unseen abuse, a quiet furious pummeling
of parts never displayed in public,
a lacy quilting of scar tissue
like a tattoo covering the whole body
isn't that enough? isn't that what it means?
our best effort sags
the dunk shot that doesn't make the rim
the poem that refuses to cry
this fragile tegument, a net shopping bag
can barely keep it in, . . . can't
it's spillling out like laundry detergent
the white granules powdering the ground
your head and skin
like K-Marts or ghosts or K-Marts
there are no ghosts not worth having
they need your rooms to rummage in
and closets and the spaces between walls
like mice, cautious, cowed, undaunted,
always forgotten, always there

BLACK LEATHER

Hotel keys turn me on
the promise of variety
purple lupine tucked
in a water-filled Coke can
inviting as a still-warm bed
We register
at the old Hollywood Roosevelt Hotel
the room clerk misses the wedding ring
beneath my black leather gloves
he smiles a smirk and hands my lover
the keys
I am a black lace woman
on the town with an unfamiliar man
I rub against you in the elevator
enjoy the slow glow that reddens your skin
bright as your ginger-colored hair

We shower together   soap each other
I stroke leather into your muscled shoulders
across your chest   your nipples grow erect
for me
you pull away   out of the water's hard spray
but I am unstoppable   continue to smooth
the soap lower   wielding it like a weapon
sudsing your solid stomach
forget the temper warning of your bright hair
your hands grip my wrists
pin them above my head
I struggle   try to twist free
you pull me taut against you
the warm water stings my spine
I look up through the fogging steam
your full mouth is a hard line

I know
you enjoy this taste of power
this hint of resistance
I'm no longer sure I know you
know any man
held there against you
my nerves open wide mouths
I don't know myself   this
craving to please
as if I were bound in black leather
as if I were owned

And I know now
nothing I allow
will be enough

nothing will be right
what you want remains
in that other room
where you'd stripped me
your clothes strewn beside mine
on the thick rug
all but that black leather belt
with its metal buckle
you'd tossed
on the smooth white bed

FACE UP

I lie a lifetime   face up
legs treading air
collect porcelain   silver
but dishwater turns gray
I wait the cheerup cocktail hour
know I carry the sea's wildness
as desert limestone carries wave patterns

Don't rock the tangible
a chorus of women's voices warns
coven of vigilant superegos
in dark hisses
their mouths drip advice
their pasts lean against me
crowd   they waver
hungers mingle with mine
and their fears are right   too

But my pen sends words that teach me
my own buried wishes are alive
survive like a reproach
the taming time long gone
I stumble on bunioned feet
leave my old body knowing
the body doesn't lie
we lie to it   make more
of the red ache   its satisfaction
can make a cage
of night's unholy cement
tie that blinds

And I am Sarah   past middle life   and bearing again
I am woman   born twice
and I wish it for you
sons   husband
wish it for you   father   depression-scarred
wish it for us all
now that I am no longer one
who can turn hungry home

I AM NO ONE

I am no one
I am anyone I want to be
Descended from daughter to daughter
I am native--I belong
I watch behind lipstick, the *chador*, sheer veils
that leap across centuries
Believe it
I can roll myself into a spinning ball
Mold mountains along my spine
Dig valleys in the hollows of my flesh
Hills and golden plains follow
my contours

My lips are warm rivers
My fluids flow, unending
Green shoots push through my pores
I draw in the sky's orange rim
Give up the umbilicus of rage
which for so long haunted me
Let the sons of Abraham quarrel
Go on using old, cramped imagery
I recite Dickinson, even Whitman
Praise whatever Druids there be
and launch myself into legend

THE HAWK STAMPS

I wish I could start under
triggers   the dog is ten miles
long   we need to organize
I strain against my clothes
rolling around   flash neon lights
the past is never the past
dead-on   dead   who do you love
most in the whole world
a smart five-year-old answers
both of you   I'm holding up
a wall   a begging bowl grows
in my toes   afraid I might live
too much   that's your send-off
sits   a lump on a bog
drop up the bottom   shuck it
why should I care
I carry my grandmother's
portable gold   inflame me
Shylock drips blood through
there's something real behind
the complaint
what the hell knock him out
with meds

INSULATION

tonight
we
watch
videos

smoke
dope

keep
time
to the
music

trace
the
slow

and
changing
contours

along
the
length

and
breadth

of
our
bodies

eat
bombay
curry

feed
each
other

slices of
cool tart
tangerines

listen
for
longings

flames
inside
us

it's
raining
hard

another
plane's
been

hijacked
in
Athens

a
friend's
husband

is
dying
of cancer

three
more
spies

just got
arrested
somewhere

* * * * * *

in
the warm
glow

of
orange
light

flesh
pleasures
flesh

we
try
to

rediscover
innocence

surrender
ourselves

* * * * * *

become
the
other

we try
to
get to

the
volcanic

the
volatile

pieces
of
ourselves

the
pieces
we keep

in hard
safe
crevices

* * * * * *

sleep
brings
us

to
our
next life

we are
a
mystery

we leave
ourselves
unsolved

ME AND MRS. MELLITSOFF

While we shop at the Plaza Market
mother meets Mrs. Mellitsoff.
I stand there squirming,
five years old, and bored.
My eyes travel along
Mrs. Mellitsoff's mountainous body,
up fatty arms, past three chins
to where my heart stops.

I interrupt their conversation:
"You know you have a mustache?"
As I finish asking the question,
I realize what I've done.

But it's too late.
Mrs. Mellitsoff's hand flies to her mouth.
"Vos hoht ahyer keend gezoght?"
"What did your child say?"

She glares at my mother, who
slaps me hard on my cheek, and
now, each time I shave *my* mustache,
I apologize to G-d and Mrs. Mellitsoff,

wondering
if I've repented
sufficiently
for telling the truth.

PEEKING AT MIRACLES

we grow brave
together
we watch
as it happens
we pull
out of our own way
we push
for the perfect poem

NAN SHERMAN

A PROPER BURIAL

He stayed in the bathroom
washing and washing,
shaving and perfuming himself,
while I lay waiting in the darkened room,
my weeping already begun.
He entered our bedroom,
smiling and fragrant.
The middle button of his pajamas
was missing.
He shoved the newspapers
onto the floor with his feet
as he climbed into bed.
When I lay my head on his chest,
the hair was still damp
and curled around my fingers.
The hands of the clock on the wall
swung in rhythm to our lovemaking.
I wanted to cover the eyes
of our children
watching us from photos
under the glass of the night table,
watching this final deception.
I hadn't yet told him I was leaving.
I don't know why.
Perhaps I wanted to give our marriage
a proper burial with all the trimmings,
a wedding in reverse,
one final weekend of being married
and all the rituals.
He smoked his cigarette
then passed it to me for the
one puff he knew I wanted.
I listened to the sound of his breathing,
coughing, rattling his newspaper,
and tried to imagine what it would be like
to have no one there on that side of the bed
and only the sound of birds.
He got up and went into the kitchen
to create his Sunday omelet,
best in Los Angeles, he bragged,
and it was.
I threw on his blue terry robe
and followed to sit on the stool,
as usual,
while he carefully sliced onions,
green pepper, mushrooms.

I watched him wipe the onion tears
onto his pajama sleeve,
watched his hand whip the eggs,
his glasses slip down his nose,
watched him,
wondering why I was doing this
pretending we were an ordinary married couple,
pretending the marriage wasn't over.

The toast burned.

MY AUNT

Memphis   wet and humid
on a summer's day.
Five years old
painting the front stoop green.
My aunt laughed, tottering on high heels.
My mother didn't, in her kitchen apron.

My aunt
smelled of jasmine perfume,
glided around the room
in silk flowery gowns,
taught me "snake hips",
her long, black hair and
hips swaying sensuously,
before I learned it was wrong.
She looked like Dorothy Lamour.

Now it's dry in Los Angeles.
A sandpiper skids along the sand
of Beverly Hills' Rodeo Drive
gamely on skinny legs,
flat rear end wobbling.

She treasures me because
I remember her
young and beautiful,
the invitation in her low laughter,
that hair,
those hips.

FIST FIGHT ON A DESERT ISLE

We could be very happy together
on a desert island
where I wouldn't nag you
to clean your room.
A house would be of no concern.
The stars would be our roof.
I wouldn't need to criticize your clothes,
if they were wrinkled or soiled.
We would wear leaves,
you would be my Adam,
I would be your Eve
in unisex dress.
I could straighten out your leaves.
I would probably want to direct the points,
a little more to the left,
then you would argue
you wanted them more to the right.
I would try to wipe them clean,
and you would scream at me
to leave your damn leaves alone
and
we might as well be living in comfort
back in Los Angeles.

RED NAIL POLISH

Time to sleep.
Red nail polish drying
pretense of youth
the one thing left to adorn
that isn't fat and wrinkled
that doesn't laugh in the mirror.

Time to dream.
Red nails to sleep
in the dark laughing
at my grey hair
covered with blond
fooling nobody.

Red nails
glowing in the dark
halloween of nails
pumpkins on fingers
mask of nails
nails of a coffin
red celebration
of a life
nailed shut.

THE EL

The elevated train screeches thru the Bronx
Clicking over years of my sleep
Under green blankets I thrust my hand-made phallus
Nylon stockings hidden by day in wooden drawers
At night, stuffing one into the other--a joystick
Silent moans hidden from brother, mother and father
Interrupted by comings and goings
Heavy steps near doors listening for sounds of my sin
Twelve-year-old Jewish girls don't go to confession
They grow fat eating guilt and chocolate cake
Making silent crosses with invisible ink
A wild stallion, my hair flying
I mount you--and feel you grow into me
Your cock plowing thru vagina, intestines, stomach
Touching my heart where we come together
Mom is standing at the bedroom door
holding a jar of chicken soup
Her apron covering breasts that milk no more
"Eat it, it's good for you"
I swallow you deep in my throat
Smiling
For once, mom is right

NIGHTMARES

I crawled into my pajamas
And curled up under the covers
Mommy kissed me good night
I said,"I love you."
I found my thumb and sucked its comfort
It lulled me to a sleep of nightmares
I awoke to a panoramic scene of murder
The walls were covered with madmen raging thru
        the house, killing and torturing
Heads were chopped off
Knives were impaled in breasts
Penises were attached to wooden poles and
        twirled wildly about
Blood was everywhere
Screams and yells filled the air
I watched in.fascination as the scene was
        replayed
Night after night, different characters
New weapons of torture
Often mommy was tortured or killed
Always there was pain and blood
And in the moring I awoke
Kissed my mother
And said, "I love you."

ALMOST TO HEAVEN

"A prostitute, that's what you are."
Black ice words
My father's mind going mad with images of tongues
        fingers, pricks in his little girl's box
The stress is tight
Real tight
Trying to please everyone--Dad, Mom, myself
Satisfying no one
So many nights of almost
Holding onto this virginity like a lifeline
Break it and die
Die
Die
Instant death or slow death but certainly death
I walk down the synagogue aisle clothed in black
Mourning the loss of what I had that really wasn't
        very much at all
The old ones rock back and forth, forth and back
Praying for my soul
It's lost, lost forever
Buried in the ashtray of the gray Chevy Impala
        covered with smoke, cigarette butts, old
        tissues, gum wrappers and condoms
The light flashes in my eyes
The cop wants to know what's going on here
"Oh, just letting our asses feel the cool night
        air, officer."
He drives away as we struggle with our clothes
You drive me home
My eyes all wild
My hair in wet strands
"Where have you been, young lady?" they want to
        know standing in the night in nightgown
        and pajamas
"Almost to heaven," I scream
"Almost to heaven."

NIGHT FRIENDS

In the dark of every night I kissed your picture hoping that this act would
        keep you alive until morning
Then I could show you and tell you what a good girl I would be
But I was only 7 and 8 and 9 and 10 and the night seemed endless
The bloody nightmares seared my sleep
The night was for blood-letting and massacres
There were no good girls in the night dreams
They became demons and witches and monsters
They brewed mysterious potions and chanted evil words
Were they hymns to the God of darkness?
These dark thoughts still live within me
They must like the home I've given them because they've never left for too
        long.

THIS IS ADDRESSED TO STEVE

anyone can be in love
driving over coated freeways.
this is to tell you all the things you
never knew about me
or maybe you did know all along.
anyone can be in love and drive.
i had a baybank express 24 card
and i got to pick my own password
my code was CHINACAT
this is what i want to tell you:
i need contact on many levels
like when you listen to that song
and you can hear two stars
dancing together
it starts with one star
then there are two
and then there are four all dancing
and sparkling in joy
but it comes back to the one star
and that star is me
because i'm dancing now by myself first,
i know you listen to China Cat
i know you have a voice that sings
my voice sings too
my voice sings when i'm driving
and i'm always in love when i drive over hills
i drive with two fingers over hills
i sing and i listen to China Cat Sunflower
i know that anyone can be in love
driving over coated diamond hills.
I wonder whether there is someone else
listening to the same song at the same time as me.
the night time is when i think of you
when i see a pine tree on the side of the road
and i compose poems
remember them until i come home
and write them down fast before i forget.
it is a talent to compose a poem
and remember it later
in jails in countries where they
won't let people write
they compose poems and books of poems and novels
they write them down when they are free.
the urge for contact springs from me in tentacles
i know you listen to China Cat
but do you know what it's like
to be in love and drive?

I CAN FLOAT THROUGH THIS ICELAND WEEKEND

there is a man outside my window
he jingles keys and moves hoses.
i walk naked in my bedroom flaunting my breasts and armpits
flaunting my sexuality
i never shave my armpits
the hair in my armpits is sexy: i have books that tell me so
it doesn't matter though because
i would never sleep with that man
he is just an audience for the hair in my armpits,
my breasts and tampon strings.
sometimes i dance naked in front of the window
i have the body of a greek statue, it's as white too
i dance slowly underneath the christmas lights
and it doesn't make sense
my stomach is full and round,
a lot of people ask me if i'm pregnant
craig says it's the clothes i wear
doris says what a stupid question
i think i'm sexy to be shaped like a greek statue
michaelangelo sculpted me as a barefoot spring maiden
full and rich and white

THANKSGIVING OREOBOY LAMENT

What if it all melted away in drips and
there were no boys no pretty boys
no oreo cookie hershey kiss boys to hope for in doorways?
What if there were no doorways to hope for
and it melted away
leaving the lines of a face,
a perfect indian, sharp and defined?
I can see it melting away
I can see her standing there exactly the same
with velvet milk energy flowing on the edges of her voice,
just like that: dressed in purple
with all of the strength and none of the excess
owning Texas in her memory,
standing there evoking the shape of Texas behind her head
and she is an indian,
it all melted away and the doors stopped reverberating with
the hopes of oreo boys that never appear.
The oreo boys like tropical fish in muffled tranquility,
the length of an eyelash:
captured swans in a garden,
tame animals who are not given names.
There are rabbits in doorways
their quivering eyes are liquid and don't rest long enough to
take me in.
Oreo bunnies, small and sweet:
they move fast without ever passing through doorways,
don't ever catch us they say.
The length of an eyelash, the softness of fur.

White rabbits pause in doorways and turn around.
Oreo boy sings songs.
Sweet Oreo Boy, I want to hate you.
Oreo Boy you make me wish I was blind,
I don't want your eyelashes in my vision.
When you shimmer in doorways I want to split your outsides and
lick away your middle and
crunch up what's left after that, get my teeth black.
Oreo Boy I want to tell you my name,
please don't go away.
Oreo Boy don't smile at me, Oreo Boy smile at me again.
Oreo Boy if I close my eyes I can see you without looking.
Oreo Boy, retreat through a doorway, leave no scent.
I want to write stories and poems,
sing songs and dance in the grass.
Oreo Boy, I want to climb a tree
and sing to you while you're sleeping.
Oreo Boy, you breathe and you are more than a painting.
I can feel your skin with my eyes,
I worship you like my own reflection in a pool.
What does it mean, Oreo Boy, to drift together in silent water
in afternoon
that crystallizes green and blue and holds us slowly
under naked sky?
Is there room to drift sideways and sing in the afternoon?
The answer doesn't matter Oreo Boy,
I am free to worship you.

GIRL

oh tell me you don't have to be a blonde
falling off
you don't have to own california
in your hair
your eyes don't have to be blue forever
who told you to laugh and fall off
imaginary shoes
point one straight finger
with one red nail
across this room
throw the head and all the hair
backwards
so he sees your red lips open
from that distance
who told you to get drunk in this place
stand and fall off
under 8 signs:
budweiser
budweiser
budweiser
budweiser
budweiser
budweiser
budweiser
budweiser

AGNIESZKA MARIA SOLTYSIK

IN ANTICIPATION OF MY RETURN TO POLAND:

Will my roots come and wait
To receive me at the gate
When I exit from the plane,
And recognize me by my name?
Will I see them on the street,
Pass me staring at their feet,
As if misplaced truths were found
By walking with eyes forced upon the ground.

Do they hang on walls
In empty reverberating halls?
Are they woven into melodies
Alllegretto and in major keys?
Or are they the sad-eyed way
Those hauting etudes should be played?

Will I find my stolen roots
In the leaden thick-soled boots
That wait at dawn with the risen dead
To buy, thank God, our daily bread,
And potatoes and a ration of meat,
Where supply and demand so seldom meet?

Dare I loook in soldier's faces,
Keep my distance at twenty paces?
Slink through crowded cemeteries
Where national heroes lie freshly buried?
Go slightly deaf when a siren cries
At the horror of averted eyes?

Will they jostle and slam
To push past me on the tram
to reach the factory on time
To pay their dues at the assembly line
With their youth and blood and sweat
Like serfs have always paid the national debt.

Or are they that special thing
In their voices when children sing
Those magic gypsy melodies
Of bloody feudal histories
That have made me never lie
About where I was born
And made men willing to die
Rather than to mourn?

A MATTER OF CULTURE

My grandfather is dying in Poland
I hope at least the T.V. works
            while they wait.
They made me promise to write often,
But I've been thinking too much,
I don't even write poems when I
            think too much.
I've resolved not to think anymore,
But now I wonder why humans can
            make absurd decisions
            so rationally.
I think perhaps that story-telling
            is a better faucet.
This is only like jumping-jacks.
Large trucks should be used to take
            better photographs
            of dead people.
Trivia, trivia, Ronald Reagan is fucking up,
And still no one's got it as good as we do
Except that everyone else knows how
            to have fun.
We just know how to party.

I KEEP TRYING TO WRITE

But it's no good
I'm going to die anyway.

Today I can do everything
But I won't. I probably won't
Even do anything except one thing
And that not even well.
This is why I keep writing.
You're going to die too.
But at least I will be able
To hold up a notebook of papers
And say~see this? I wrote this.
This is what I have done. And this guy?
This sucker actually read all of it
While he could have been doing something
Constructive. Like pounding nails.
Or cutting wood.

IT ALWAYS TURNS OUT SO NEGATIVE

I saw a black rabbit
Running across the snow
And my father shot at it
And missed.
He looked at me and yelled
That there was a rabbit behind me
And why did I always have to be in the way?

FROM A FORMER LIFE

              my master is
                        a woman
she hides inside
                a heron
                    the sails
                             are full
               the wind and the poppy
forcing opium
                down
                  their
                    throats
              my round eyes
look into her
                  thousands of years
the world is born again
                  and it never ends
waves
      light   water
                  watch the reflection
IT is all the same
                  when will it be my turn
            to lie on my back
                    in yin simplicity
taking yang bullshit
                  learn that they
            consider sperm
                is ¢
      because it swims
                  our egg
                is -
        because it waits
                  our egg waits
              because it is scared
knows that
         the yang light brings life

SLEEPING IN THE REPTILE HOUSE

the old dragon's dead
but we saved his sperm
and slide it into the female
that wanted nothing to do
with him when he was alive
the joke's on her
it's nice to run the world
so few of us get the chance
I take Charlie and Lilly out for a swim
in my pool
Charlie's indigo body glides through the water
his forked tongue tasting the chlorine
Lily floats suspended in the deep end
I dry her off
wrap her boa body
all cream and chocolate
around my neck
the noose is tight
the guillotine sharp
which is quicker
the jerk or the slice
how fast can the soul leave the body
no use hanging around this trash
the only solution is devil's island
a quiet place to retire
with the murderers and rapists
paradise among the scum
I stay in the reptile house
they know enough to leave me alone
I am busy breeding dragons
swimming with snakes
and wrestling crocodiles
the killers worry about me
they make such good food
the rapists are not so tasty
and don't fight as much
being natural cowards
better to feed them to lazy lazy snakes
I have to clean the moat this week
the algae is taking over
I can't see the piranhas
they get the left overs
tomorrow I take the dragon eggs
to the mainland
maybe I can finally get a date
they all laughed at me in high school
just wait until they see me
at the class reunion
with my dragon on the leash
they'll know I mean business
they'll pay attention
or I'll put them on the menu.

CARESS

you are a river
we become a bridge over
as you change
to the ocean

we are the tide
the moon   the breeze
moving across the beach
shifting the sand
placing each grain
in a slightly different
position

we hold each other
tight
we are rhythm
a cloud
expanding across
the sky   the blue
that is transparent

is nothing

POPE JOAN

you know I am an artist
you have seen my sketches
read the entries
in my diary
the rain in my room
will not stop until I learn to float

I hide at McDonald's
sleep in my Toyota
call myself Jim
lucky sixes roll me flat
I can't breathe with the dice on top of me

I will not worship her anymore
POPE JOAN   POPE JOAN
you hid your pregnancy
took my sperm and ran between my testicles
I will not forgive
I will find you and take what is mine
remind you of my devotion
climb inside you
worm in fruit
digging through and sucking you out from inside
I am done
I am Wayne
I can breathe

THE INTERVIEW

Jose Jiminez - Is that your true name?
Are you known by any other names?
Is "Stilletto" your gang name?
Is that why you have a tattoo of a dagger
On the inside of your forearm?
It says here that you are twelve.
Is that correct?

Jose, do you know why you are here?
That's right - because of that boy.

How much money did you and your brother
steal from that boy. The report says his
Mother gave him $1.36 to buy eggs
at the market. Is that about right?

Jose, why did you take the boy's money?
To buy candy?

I look at Jose. I see no emotion
In his eyes. I look past him. I see myself
As a boy his age. I grew up poor
also. I shared the same bed with my sister.
My parents slept in the living room
I remember wanting . . . wanting even candy
And having no money.

I look at Jose. He thinks he is tough.
He comes from a tough neighborhood ruled by
the Blythe Street gang
If you ever wanted to know what "machismo" means
I wouldn't bother to explain
I would just point to Jose.

I drove by my old neighborhood last week
The apartment house still has an eight foot high
Chain link fence surrounding it
Topped off with three strands of barbed wire
I was never sure if it was designed
To keep them out or to keep us in

We were poor also. I remember Saturday
Mornings walking up and down the alleys. I would
Rummage through the garbage looking for
Returnable coke and beer bottles. I would exchange
Them at the liquor store for two cents each

I would buy a licorice stick. Sometimes I found
        Enough bottles to go to the Empire Theater
On Pico or the Westlake Theater on Alvarado across
        From MacArthur Park.

        Yet I never felt good about what
I was doing to get money. I learned then
        What I know now
Sometimes you simply do whatever it is
        You think you have to do
Regardless how you feel about it

        One day I learned that the Herald
Newspaper was looking for a paper boy to take
        Over the corner at Hoover
And Olympic Boulevard. They were looking
        For a boy fourteen or older.
I was twelve. But I needed to get out
        Of the garbage
I needed to feel better about myself
        So I lied.
But I was short for my age
        They didn't believe me
I argued, but I didn't beg. I needed the job.
        They gave me a chance.

        They gave me thirty papers to sell
I sold twenty at the corner. I went out into
        Rush hour traffic and hawked five
Papers while the cars were stopped for the red light
        Then I decided to hit the bars

        I will never forget walking into one bar
A drunk was sitting at the bar reciting a poem.
        Something to do with the shooting
Of a man by the name of Dan McGrew, I recall.
        The bartender saw me standing there listening
He yelled, "Get the hell out of here, you punk."
        The drunk said, even louder, "Let the poor
Kid sell his newspapers, for Christ's sake."

        I sold the rest of the newspapers in the bar.
On the way out, I looked at the drunk. He looked at me.
        We didn't say anything to each other.
Just exchanged a kind of "knowing" look; you see,
        The drunk was my Dad.

        Jose, according to the arrest report, at first,
The boy refused to give you his money, is that correct?
        What did you do when he refused?
You gave him a bloody nose? What did you next do?
        Jose, what did you next do?
Jose, look at me when I am talking to you.
        What did you next do?

You don't know what I mean? Well, according
To the autopsy report, the coroner claims the boy was
        Tortured to death.
How do you feel about that? Jose just sits in silence.
        No emotion. No remorse. Nothing.

        While I wait for a response from Jose,
I remember my first killing. It was when I was
        Attending Hoover Street grammar school.
We were studying metamorphosis. I would search
        The lantana flower bushes looking
For caterpillars. I would find them and put them
        Into a mayonnaise jar. Inside the jar
I would put a twig and some lantana leaves. I
        Punched holes in the lid with an ice pick
So the caterpillar could have air. Then I
        watched and waited. The caterpillar soon
Anchored itself to the twig with a sticky substance.
        Then he would begin to spin a cocoon. After
Awhile the cocoon would get hard and dark brown.
        At about that time, the cocoon would break
Open and a butterfly would emerge. I wanted to
        Keep the butterflies but they would beat
Their wings against the glass jar attempting to fly.
        I was afraid they were hurting themselves
So I let them go free. I wanted to learn more about
        Butterflies. I went to the public library
At Lafayette Park. I learned that some men. . .
        Even great men were not letting the butterflies
Go free. They were collecting and mounting them
        Between panes of glass.

        I remember my first instincts told me
This was wrong. I didn't want to kill a butterfly
        Yet it was civilized.
So, one day, I picked up a straight pin and pressed
        It firmly down into the skull
Of the butterfly. But it didn't die like it was
        Supposed to according to the books.
It began to move. It staggered across the
        Kitchen table, falling down occasionally on
One or more of its spindly legs, then rising again,
        Slower each time.
I began crying. I had only wounded the butterfly.
        I removed the pin and pressed it back into
The butterfly's skull, again and again. My eyes
        Filled until the butterfly was a blur and I

Couldn't see to find its skull anymore. Then, finally,
        The butterfly stopped moving
And I was released from its grip on my throat.

        I never captured butterflies again. I thought
I would never kill again. I was wrong. The paratroopers

And a War changed all that. I learned what Jose
knew: You can kill, if you can suppress your feelings.
        Besides, in War killing is civilized like
        The killing of butterflies.

        I look at Jose through the iron bars.
He reminds me of a helpless dog I once saw locked up
        In a County Animal Shelter. Like Jose
The dog had been physically abused at home. The dog
        Would growl and snap at anyone close.
I learned if nobody adopted the dog within three days
        He would be destroyed. I wanted to reach out
And pet him. Lie to him. Tell him everything was
        Going to be allright.

        What shall I say to Jose? I can't lie to him.
He is going to be found guilty of murder in the first degree
        And sent to prison. Even if he survives, he is
Still going to be destroyed, bit by bit. I want to
        Reach out and touch him. I would like to get his
Attention. Take him away from the lock up to where we
        Can both smell the flowers . . . away from the
Garbage, the gangs, the drunken fathers, the violence . . .

        Then I want to tell him something. I want to tell
Him that he is still young enough to change . . . to learn
        About love and compassion and forgivenesss
That these are feelings that can be learned like a song
        That can be learned; but, I have yet to learn all
The words to that song myself and, for now, the melody
        Escapes me

CINCO HERMANAS VAGABUNDAS

Cinco mujeres . . . cinco hermanas vagabundas
       laughing together in a topless green jeep
across the Mexican selva virgen, passing
       pregnant mules, color of coffee beans,
and skinny white horses and
       fat black hogs with floppy ears.

Smell of burning in the air-
       burning trash,
       burning excrement,
       burning short dry weed grass
in charcoal patches on vacant desert lots,
       burning under the jungle sun,
the same burning smell of India, of
       dry grass huts and palm frond rooftops
the same wherever they are....
       the smell of simplicity,
       the rudiments, and
      a sudden richness
whose scent will fill you up
for years to come, like the milk
of the split wide open coconuts
whose green and brown and
       hacked in half husks
litter the beaches of Rincon de Guayabitos
               in piles,
where las cinco hermanas vagabundas
walk together across the sinking sand
       singing
of companeros & felicidad, of
       loyalty and passion
       Il Corazon....

Looking up across the waves to the
       Island of the Sacred Heart; it rings
with the screams of pelicanos
       whose stark white guano covers
boulders, vines and iguanas, smothering
       every cove and crevice with a
pungent white crust that blows up in the dust clouds
       across the brown feet and white palms
               of the sisters
       who crash through dead underbrush,
struggling up dried bone waterfalls, proving....
       what? That Heart is Sacred, Enduring;
       that Laughter is their Strength; that their
       Blood soaking into the white sand together
               their Bond.

And somewhere in the jungle, the
                    mountains, the sea,
the birds will call the names of
          five sisters, the snakes will
prepare a path for them through the desert,
          knowing the print of their feet, the
turtles will carry their weight whenever they
          grow too tired to fight the waves....
and one fine day, the trees will shake
          and loosen the soil around their roots
to make a welcome place
                              for their graves.

THE REDHEAD

The redhead has visions of overthrowing Amazonia. The waters of
that ancient river stretch, in his mind, from Southmost America to
his pelvic muscles, not necessarily in that order. Crossing only
white America, and certain caucasian outlands, he openly despise
the spiks, wops, niggers and chinks, and would pound your face to
turkey shit if you mentioned "jew" with a slur . . .
(He wears a yarmulka for Pasach, then pins it to the dog; it is the
poetic license of prejudice to be inconsistent and ego-specific.)

At fifteen he tried to rape the Jamaican housekeeper, his penis all
trussed up in surgical gauze. I caught them struggling on her bed
between the ironing and the outgoing shirts, spilt windex on her
uniform, blue piss. He grabbed his erection, the sacred jewel, and
ran off as if expecting someone to snatch it. (His wily worm held
no more interest for me than the neighbor boy's, who paid me a
quarter when I was eight to shine a flashlight on it while he stood
drop-drawered in his closet.) The redhead's did, however, look in-
finitely funnier, announcing itself to the world that way, all done
up in its holey turban.

He threw knives at me like the circus daredevils on T.V., but with
no practice arena and no intentions of missing. He shot hockey
pucks off my head, three sticks at a time, and once strangled me
to blue-faced unconsciousness in front of the babysitter (who quit
shortly thereafter). Cement glue missed my face but claimed my
hair, which I resented the cutting of until I read that Joan of Arc
was 'close-cropped.'

He leaves death threats on my bed nights, when he comes to visit.
 Female pornography decorates my windshield. I examine the
door his single kick has burst the latch from, while my mother still
shakes her head softly behind me, sighing, "Don't complain, dear
. . . he only wants *attention*."

TURN ABOUT IS FAIR PLAY

I don't give myself away anymore.
   I give what you Give--
      Sweetcakes, wines & cheeses,
   compliments like powdered sugar
      to make you smile-
And you do smile . . .

You think it odd and Interesting--
   and awkward when you
      can't come Inside.
When I've spent some time
   Inside you,
      we'll Talk.

WINDOW

I love nothing so much as
sitting before the window at night,
      writing,
staring at my reflection in the
darkened pane.

PAULA THOMPSON

ST. JOAN SITS AT MY FEET

incoherent in discussion
with the blue virgin that
spins like a dragonfly

caught in the web
the unmoving air of
heat and love.

We can believe in anything
they have to throw at us

the zen master brushes the
fence with darkness
and even this I absorb

in this flesh
are expectations of survival
this incoherent self

this is what I
have to work with
finding God
finding home
finding a man
or truth

at my feet
is Joan of Arc

God is spoken every day
by such stranded souls

burned because the mother
answered for Him
mother of God save me
from my need for consistency

I believe there is a mother
but was God conceived

Did Joan scream
or was she silent

it's a slow flame etches the skin
a line at a time

if you're to be burned
choose the biggest fire.

THE BUTCHER'S WIFE

When winter hits the Irish coast the Brenner pass
the boot of Italy
when winter hits
and there's no wood
no turf to burn
no bread

paint the butcher's wife
give her pink nipples

to look us dead in the eye with
the butcher's wife stuffed with fragrant
herbs and crumbs
the apron stained with
fruits from the pie she bakes in the oven
background left side

the fowl the venison
lying on the table

Rodin looks at feet
hands of important men
gives them foundations rock like
earth bound such feet such hands

this last winter
when the food runs out
he wears old socks cut to fit around
his hands while he works the stone.

Peace in the houses of silver of gold of fur
taken off boats
that sail the Mediterranean
taking prizes

Rembrandt paints the fat man
with his foot on a small
trunk of ivory
his plumed hat and pursed lips
insolent

The artist stands back
twelve feet for vision
for perspective for protection for isolation
behind the glass of the Metropolitan
the Whitney
the Norton Simon
these last days of winter.

BAG LADY MOON

Who builds a room
with the light so high
the elevator womb
can't get you close enough.

Watch out
the Bag Lady Moon descends
lays her dark skirts over your head

for what are you punished
the old woman who stood
all the way to the ocean
on the bus while you
read Dante

and contrary to the illusionary day
the lute in the hand
ghoul pallor against chestnut stained rain.

Only a blind man builds a room
without light
but if he is mad
the light is just beyond reach.

Basket born basket ride to death
wrapped in the cellophane
you are still
female, woman, mother

remember the drift of days
cutting patterns to fit
the life you dream

the scent of sweat, Madame Rochas perfume,
Lysol and lemon wax rubbed into the wounds.

Whirl on lady bride
time's cup at your lips.

Everything must be in place or
it's the street for me
join the ones who surrender
how peaceful to sit wherever
you find yourself
wrapping your skirts around your legs

Soon you are a heap
covered with dog hair, fleas the
stench of cat in your nose
a witch's fingers
cup your chin.

When I go I'll take only
what I wear

so weary
the only way to
listen to the music
is to stop

I don't need to play
the daybreak
or hush the night sky.

TELL ME WHAT MIND IS

why
three specific
breaths

taken this day
are unforgettable.

how loud was the
collision
of planets

whose ear
could hear it.

CAROL BRIDGE WALKER

IN YOUR ANGLES HOUSE

In your glass house
with its glass tables
the view you eat is the sea,
past the glass room that houses
the pool, where sometimes you must
swim.

At the luncheon where we are all
pressed and clean, the napkins,
navy blue linen, spread
over our laps, you mention
how in matters of justice
you like the vigilante role.

We've already covered the
future of your special church
and the good income of everyone here;
now you tell us the dangers
of not enough punishment,
and mention China where

two men were executed right after
they'd robbed the shop, a method
almost eliminating crime in China.
Your right fist makes a large
red place on your left palm, I
notice your slim surgeon fingers.

The long-haired boy of seventeen
at the opposite end of the table
says he likes to think that
since he wasn't killed during
the robberies he committed
when he was addicted to drugs,

that now he can help some people
get over their drug problems.
You half clear your throat with words,
saying the rule might not
apply in all cases; your neck
does not bend, you stare at nothing and
chew the poppy seed cake.

LISTEN

it's all right to be this crazy
if the spinning won't stop
goes so fast no one
notices I'm spitting grapefruit
seeds into their
back pockets
don't tell them trees
will grow from my lust, leaves
can either stand or
tumble but it's got to be
fast

listen
I am touching you
but my palms have held
roses
        calculators, I
figure the intensity
of sun
this jumping I'm in
spells more innocence than we
have known
hunger
the taking in pure, there
is no abstract food
touch me

MOTIF

In the beginning--tatting and crocheted collars from the attic--
my grandmother had an idea of innocence like the child she was,
if the collar fit the dress she could go where she needed:
to the church, in the choir, to meet a man she could marry.
A child born--if it died--might change things,
but a house on a street with enough trees would keep standing.
And if the child she borrowed from a woman who couldn't
but then wanted her back in a couple of years--also died, after
she returned her--she might grow thinner.
If the daughter who was finally born was not the girl she'd
loved those two years, she could still love her some
and always fear losing her.
This daughter who grew up might never be quite sure
of her dresses or collars, or where to hide from people knowing
something about her which she couldn't discover herself.
This one waited years to have a daughter she thought would complete her,
whom she would fear losing, who would write very small stories
about women who hold on to what they have lost.

THIS ROOTING HERE

Kangaroos are important
discipline isn't what we're after
tails flying them
originality is needed
a gopher doesn't do this
even giraffes miss the high flight
of early morning;

bamboo bends all the way to the ground
but an arc isn't an intention,
it's perception,
night looks innocent as a doe named
Jacqueline
pinned on the line with sunflowers,
day complex as cheese
stuck after the metal cools;

we trim ourselves innocent as toenails,
unbought as the root flowers
in their crystal shadows,
begun again and unseparate as the red
stripe on Methuselah's spinning top.
Don't doubt the sun that never burns
and lays itself gold
in pool rounds,
the lily carried green
to its source;

begin the spelling like this
unzipping from behind
never meeting in the front,
begin the telling with frogs
stuck on their heads in mud,
their feet flying like
successful flags;
make the panorama real,
trees pressing thumbs
into the deluge sky.

BETSEY WARWICK

MOON WANDERINGS

at 5 O'clock
the moon sat
on the crest
of the hill
so big and
chalky and
bizarre looking
it was hard
to tell it
was the moon

what amazed me
was the speed
with which
it climbed
clearing the
mountain
within minutes
hanging like
a lantern
an alter ego

Freud's cancer-
ridden jaw

he prophesied
he would die
at 40
then at 60
endured till 90

the pain
the mess
the cocaine
the dribbling food

my grandfather
had it too
it ate his
blond handsomeness
from his throat
to the lower portions
of his face
this prosperous Jew
who travelled from
Odessa to Berlin
for treatment

and never saw
the country where
his children
grew old
and died

I am a sandwich
between two cultures
Suzanne's white coffin
pink and yellow
roses of her youth
24 years old
copper haired
she taught aerobics
at the hospital
where they
pronounced her dead
her life the
prerogative of
a drunk driver

"and she who
was always last
is first"

I held Pat
in my arms
beside the
open grave
her grief
flowed into me

college thirty
years ago

memories come
like pilgrims
to the altar

she lived there
I was just
a "day hop"
(even the name
was demeaning)

I can hear
it raining
like a
pissing cow

crossing the road
in England
morning dripping

grey and green
traffic stopped
on all sides
while the herd
took their pleasure
nice to be
a cow

wandering like
the moon

ROOTS AND CANDLES

For Msgr. Pollard

cut a turnip
and insert
a red candle
burn it in the
window of
every house
in this land
of roots
and thistles

rural Ireland
Christmas Eve
this signal-
studded night

". . .that there
is room in
that house"

room at
the inn
and room in
the heart

and you
telling it
still burning

NEW ORLEANS CEMETERY

they bury
their dead
above the ground
shield them
from high water

generation
after generation
under one roof

they make
good neighbors
despite
close quarters
they keep
the peace

small houses
from which
no inhabitant
strays

TRANSPLANT

a seed
that dies

a man bicycling
east to west
to Stanford
for a checkup

a dead man's heart
pumping
in his chest

TICKING AWAY

I am ticking away
when I'm swimming, eating
or dreaming,
I'm still ticking.
He is not.
Yesterday I was 24.
Today I'm 32.
I see crow's feet
nesting around my eyes,
tiny wrinkles crease my lips,
even when I'm not smiling.
My breasts are as firm as
sweet sixteen,
still waiting to nurse my child.
I can pull the skin on my back
away from my bones,
My bones, sometimes they crack
when I bend to pet Farfel.
He can wait 5 years, 8 years
even 10 years to raise a family.
I cannot.
Maybe I can't wait at all for him.
He calls me honeybun
110 pounds of fun.
Last night he stayed at my home
studying while I went to see
"My Other Husband" *en francais.*
I came home with a raspberry tort
that we licked off each other's lips.
He wanted to tuck me in bed before
he finished reading.
So he picked me up and carried me
step by step up the stairs.
I shut off the light
with my big toe.
He threw me on the
satin sheets and
sighed out of breath.
He lit the charcoaled wick
of the honeycomb candle.
I am still ticking away.
He loves to see my white lace
lingerie dangle from the
brass lamp
and his briefs are always
hiding somewhere between the

sheets.
He doesn't know
Matisse
Gertrude Stein
nor Van Gogh,
And he doesn't know
my middle name is Adele,
And he doesn't know
I've written this poem,
ticking away,
ticking away.

LETTERS

I sit in the kitchen,
stare at the empty carton
of strawberry yogurt,
the kind already mixed.
The oil lamp is not lit
and hot water whistles.
I look at the stamp on the
torn white envelope.
A bedouin woman
cloaked in red
with dangling earrings,
necklace and anklets
stands of Kufic lettering
La Marsa, Tunisia.
He lives in a villa overlooking
the clear Mediterranean
and ten years later,
is still sending me letters.

PERPIGNAN

Five years old, living in Perpignan,
through deep snow she walked to school,
past La Boulangerie.
The air smelled of baguettes and buttery croissants.
Monsieur Renaud stood at the corner of the Gothic Church
comme tous les jours, selling hot chestnuts for 60 centimes.
Before History was over, Madame Juillet put a potato
in a wood burning stove.
She cupped the heated potato in her hands,
to keep her warm,
on her cold walk home.

MINIATURE HORSES

Miniature horses pulled the sleigh
through soft snow.
Moon crisps lit our path,
ting ting ting in the night's stillness.
Nordic Kings wrapped in thick wool blankets,
Gaylord sang Camelot's repertoire.

Approaching a log cabin the silence stopped.
The foyer ignited by fireplaces
Hot sheepherders bread and red wine
warmed our bellies.
Klaus' accordion fingers played
"La Vie en Rose,"
White candles silhouetted laughing faces,
"She'll be comin' round the mountain when she comes . . ."

Mitzi stared at the spinach stuffed rabbit
soaking in orange liquor.
Thought of those black kids in Pittsburgh
selling skinned rabbits
up and down Ralph Road.
Her stomach squeezed her throat,
"God I can't eat this."

Oh my darlin'
Oh my darlin' Clementine
You are lost and gone forever . . ."

When I was 13 I stood before my bedroom mirror
wanting to see what I would look like when I grew up.
Would I be pretty and tall. Would I really grow breasts.
Maybe I would even visit Paris. Who would I marry and are
4 kids too many?

Now the horses wait by the window
but can't stand still.
None of us can stand still when we're waiting,
none of us.

I WENT TO THE BALL

and I wore a red
dress, a thin silk sheath
that wrapped my body
like a Bing cherry
you couldn't stop staring
bought me a beer   spilled
it   your young face was
so red   wiping wet
beer from my thighs   you
promised to buy me
a new dress   we danced
and we danced till we
married   I hung my
red dress in the hall
closet   we stayed home
and had a baby
the sweet grape of our
love   showed her to our
friends   my mother tied
red ribbons to her
carriage   to protect
her from the evil
eye   one day I came
home and my red dress
was gone   you gave it
to cousin Faye   a
brassy blonde   she lived
across the street   I
no longer slim or
cherry   switched to earth
tones   quit dancing   cursed
my blood   waited years
to know   you could not
strip that second skin
away   red silk still
hangs secretly in
me   a small brush fire
on the edge of a
civilized city
where we meet again
faces shielded by
masks   bodies concealed
under animal
skins   still red   still wet

COME, LET US CONFOUND THEIR LANGUAGE

Genesis XI, 7

The Jews of Fairfax
are darker this year.
Familiar Yiddish
mingles with other tongues:
Persian, Moroccan, Russian;
mingles with the
bearded young Chabadniks
who have seen everything:
dope addicts, Jesus freaks,
even a woman
who defies sex taboos
and is asking for books
explaining the Kabbalistic mysteries.
Storekeepers are wary.
Their black nervous eyes
watch for gypsies
and fair-haired adolescents.
At night I dream
my father calls to tell me
my mother is dead;
she won't keep her date
to go shopping with me.
I don't cry
because I already know she is dead.
In the dream and out,
she has lived her time.
In her time,
the Jews of Fairfax were white,
their skin and their hair were white,
and she understood
what they were afraid of:
sticks at the ends of words,
broken glass,
and never knowing exactly
when to pack.

BREAKING HABITS

Maybe it's better to go the back of a cave alone.
Scratch rage or leach the spectrum from vegetables,
paint animal worship on the walls.
All my life I've answered as if I had to.
Dense selected sentences
woven around the seed, nuanced
like ripening peaches:
fiber, transparency, flavor, skin.
Some I ate,
gave some away,
and stayed hungry.

If love is guaranteed
can I learn to be

still, so all of motion and stasis
can meet in the throw of the coins
which I no longer have to carry?
Still, so the chance pattern
of milkweed filament landing
need never again be mysterious.
Still, so the Fool in the deck
is free to fall off the cliff
in the wind's direction.

Maybe it's better to measure the length of this beach alone.
First in the morning
to step off land's perimeter.
To study the sea lives stranded here.
To count only on the inevitable appearance
of dogs, husks, and wreaths of kelp.
To stop looking in your cards
for answers.

PERILOUS

Once I got in the habit of walking
with small stones in my hand, rubbing them
like bells, savoring them
with an uncontrollable smile, the invisible
telling its shape, I could hold that
instead of fear.
I want to say, I know shape
isn't what it seems to be, it's only
container, blood does live in stones.
Even as I write, my palm
at the percept of cold slick surface
comes alive, almost immersed in an icy
stream. My feet become used to
slippery passage.
I want to say, this arises from
tapping, stone against stone,
but it really unfolds from story.
It was my mother lived on a moving stream,
stored wrapped meat in the flow to keep
fresh, crossed it barefoot and young.
Nothing was slippery then,
everything brimming,
America undreamed. The pebbles I find
in the gutter, at the curb, small worn
shards of river rock, decorate these
suburban lawns, in orderly patterns.
Sprinklers wash them into the street.
I pass by, pick up two,
roll them like dice. Whatever comes up.

"SNIFFLES AND A FULL HEAD"

Sniffles and a full head
soup sipped from under
the blankets
spread with dolls
half-dressed
the pajamas twist
and turn
the button's too tight
she brings
more soup.
I'm sniffling again
I want marrowbone attention
instead I get
canned soup
jazz on the radio
and magazines
and books
spread across the covers
my tee shirt twists
around my neck
The pillow's hard
I can't sleep
the soup's only warm
maybe tea will help
the apartment ads
are in gray
the newsprint marks my fingers
and smudges on the sheets
I found those
dolls in a
blue and white polka dotted
cardboard suitcase
a sheath of pink corduroy
sashed with green satin
criss-crossing plastic
breasts and circling
the waist
another wears green lace
with seed pearls
the work of my
nine-year-old fingers
sitting alone under
the sloping eaves next to
my attic bedroom
scraps of fabric
and lace and a
broken pearl necklace

a package of silver sequins
thread too rough for the lace
tiny tucks so the moire
would drape across
the plastic body with
the nylon hair
tucked away in a cardboard suitcase
with silver stars pasted
onto the polka-dot surface
the carpet left ridges
in my legs
tweed bumps
make her pretty
dressing the doll
in dreams of lace
and pearls and satin
with nine-year-old
tweed knees folded
under me monklike
the afternoon sun
pools through the west window
and I move
the books are for
darker spaces
tucked with a flashlight
under the covers
I want to be Nancy Drew
ask questions
discovered
lights out
I lie in the dark
the window won't quite shut
and the air crawls through
the rafters are ribs
and the house
wheezes
I fall asleep with
my face to the wall

"I'M LYING ON THE COUCH"

I'm lying on the couch,
my feet propped up.
A green fireplace
needs to be here
like in the old
apartment
weeds where I would
sit and sometimes
write surf
My first place
had no fireplace

just light from hills
and my space
tethered to the
highways where I travel
car speeds along
camera on the seat
lie back at the rest stop
dream of seeing
life in the lens
my first camera
was a brownie with
rolls of film
hand-fed trout
held up
caught in a pond
where they had no escape
water plants hit by
sunlight in a stream
moss trickles through trees
rotting trunks
returning to earth
worms wriggle
home soil
dreams of hooks
screams
an eight-year-old's fingers
thread him on sharp points
picket fence
sharpened stakes to fall
against while climbing
out

PROP WASH

The prop wash
of the fan
that hum that sounds of skies
and wings and flight
away from here
to the edge of wherever I left
myself
when I rode the lightning
to this house with the half-finished air
riding the edge of
undone
not done
flour, water
unleavened life
rising in me
the acid at the back of my throat
swallowed again
making furrows

gagging
choking on what I've swallowed
and can't give up
prop wash
caressing my face
a mother's hands on a child's face
fevered air
burning
crashed wings
useless for flying
they make struts
for a new structure
right makes flight
kitty hawk
chicken hawk
selling the dream
and the nightmares
ridden not flown
rising like yesterday's meal
gone sour

MICHELE WILLIAMS

EVERYTHING WOULD BE THE SAME
WITHOUT STUART

I knew Doris would serve chicken.
She always served chicken.
There would be small portions,
little wine and
I would be hungry
before I went to sleep.

I knew her house would be spotless,
the floors, heavy with shine,
brass door knobs polished
until they melted.
I would think of my house
and wish I were neater.

There would be baskets
of yellow mums.
The table would be set by 3:30.
We would eat at 9:00.
Almost everything with Doris
would be the same
except for Stuart.

Stuart had grown up.
He was writing poetry,
rapping poetry,
for musician friends,
performing locally.
The only white boy
in the group,
his latest poem was
about equality.

Something about how his body,
felt the music.
Something about his hair,
how it lay so close to his head
and then exploded, said
Stuart would be different.

I wanted to tell him
everything I knew,
give him every poem.
I wanted to listen
self-consciously
half the night
until he had tired.

I wanted to know
if Doris would mind.
I talked with him so long.
Did it fit into her plan,
her yellow mums?
Later, she thanked me.

What a strange thing to say,
thank you.
Thank you for talking
to Stuart.

FOREPLAY

I am lying here holding myself,
trying not to feel cold,
when he reaches over to me
and puts his arm under my neck
to pull me closer to him
against him in the late darkness
before we go to sleep,
before his arm goes to sleep
cradled under my head,
and his back begins to hurt
because of the unusual position
on the water bed.

He winces and I ease my face away
until I feel my night cream
pull at his chest hairs
and my nose start to run
because of the plants blooming
under the window sill,
while the wine has made me wheeze
and I begin to cough hard
catching my breath and
stifling the sharp jab
I feel in my shoulder
from the bursitis
they discovered yesterday.

I cannot hold my position on top
of his arm a minute longer
so I carefully unfold myself
to answer the three or four pangs
I feel in the other parts of my body,
leaving him free to adjust himself
to the sagging bed
so he feels his back pain less
and my shoulder gives me peace.
He sighs and I sigh and
I wonder what we have accomplished.

MY DINNER WITH JOSEPH

I am eating gazpacho
at Joseph's round oak table
when, suddenly, I see a tall woman
carrying a bear on her shoulders.
The bear is young, a bronze bear,
with hair shined cold into furrows.
The woman has parted her hair
into thick plaits that cover
the bear's haunches
and hold her breasts in place.
Her skirt is long
and her face is fine.

I know this woman.
She has a bear on her back
and she is carrying him
into the forest.
I know this woman, but
I don't know the bear.
I don't know what she
will do with the bear.

He is a heavy bear, a male
and he is on her back
to hurt her.
With straight claws,
he will cut her.
First he will make love with her,
then he will eat her.

This bear is a loving bear.
He wants to marry her,
to have two
bear-like children who will
fulfill a dream she had
about a bear
who had bear cubs
with a woman.

The woman is not as lovely
as she seems.
Her teeth are longer and sharper
than the bear's.
They will tear his skin off
and place his skull
at the table.
She will eat this bear
in the face.

They are walking into the forest
to play on the crushed redwood.
She will thrust her slim fingers

under his fur.
He will hold her
and berries will drip
from their lips.

I don't think they will
die together, but I don't know
how their story will end.
There are so many stories
so many different stories
about the woman and the bear.
I don't know which is the right story.
I don't even know which one
is the woman.

I look at Joseph.
His girl-face smiles at me,
at the table, at the sculpture.
Which one is the woman?
Is it Joseph?
Is it Joseph, the one
who selected the table
and prepared it until the dark oak
shined smooth. I know him
but I don't know
what he will do with the bear.
There are so many different stories.

It's because I know the woman,
but I don't know the bear.
There is so much I don't know.
Sometimes I can't even speak
the little I know.
Sometimes I forget.
I ask too many questions.
I should make up a story,
one story ˙ and not think
of the many different stories.
I should make up one story and
I should tell it.
But would it be about
Joseph or the bear?

GOOD BYE

Today I bought some hanging plants
for the front.
It made me ridiculously happy
to plant them.
I love flowers.
I usually kill everything I plant
unfortunately.
I will probably kill these.
But, meanwhile,
they make me happy.

There's something about things that grow
that knocks me out.
Out of dirt and sun
comes a big, succulent orange,
or sweet smelling gardenias,
or brilliant azaleas.
Right out of dirt and sun.
The sun energizes those electron orbits
into excitation.
Leaping around
turning nitrogen and carbon and hydrogen
into fruits and flowers.
If that can happen

what can't?

And that's not even the most
remarkable thing.
Animals moving around on feet
and hooves
or with wings and flippers,
all with their own separate consciousness.

It's very beautiful
when you think about it.

As a human
I have separated myself
from the animal, vegetable.
I am unnatural.
My activities are meaningless
suited to nothing.

Except, maybe, reproduction.
Now that's certainly natural

even in the most unnatural
circumstances.
Right now
it's kicking inside
and I can't believe
this little blastomere
is going to go for it.
Out of sun and dirt
once removed.

DRONES

When I lay down to sleep last night
I thought of all the men I'd known
in the biblical sense
Their star scent still seemed to be on me
though I suspect I don't even remember
all those bumble bees

It seems to me now
that then
people adored me
a salt shaker with a loose lid
cocaine.
Especially these men I think of
starting with boys and mirrors.
They thought I was kick the can athletic
and witty and charming
as crystal candlesticks
in the sunlight
like Pollyanna's prisms
throwing rainbows.
In short
I thought, grey thunderclouds,
I owned the world

But now
as I lay in bed I know
amplifiers and guitars and midget musicians
that I've lost it
my fifty cent beer scent.
Sent it away with my choices
or buried it in my work
so it couldn't breathe
on the sundeck
by the lake.

I pull at the neck of my turban
and a coiled cobra
with a full neck of his own
looks me in the eye.

Cold snake eye.
He will enter me
through the mouth
or magic carpet
and coil in my guts
ready to put out
the lamp.
Maybe it's a homecoming.
A crown will appear on my head
like it used to.
But now it can't guard me or
the crown jewels,
since I'm dead inside.
Bitten by the cobra
Stung by the bee.

ME AND MY WOMB

I never was
or wanted to be
the kind of girl
who sat around and waited
patiently

As a child I ran fast
on hard dust in Texas
blinded by hot white glare
and heartbeat dreams
of Apache warriors
and mustangs black and white
and wild and loving
only me.

And then came breasts
and uneasiness
and awkward and frantic
in body
unable to forget the length of arm crashing
into lamps and desks,
the painful eyeball stares of
other romping beings
seeming quite unlike myself
and myself one of them.

But even then
I kept moving
into dust devils
jeep wagoneers
rare air
I was going somewhere
but I was afraid
I couldn't take me with me.

Now I am learning to wait
patiently
like my mother did
and all the other women.
Nine months at least
of strange centeredness.
A calm made of the smell
of faint perfume, faint music
strong earth and soil.
My belly ties me to the earth
my mother
and myself, and tenderness
and for once I have caught up with me
and we all sit here waiting.

POET'S BIOS

Christine Palmer Allen is the publisher and editor of *Blue Window* magazine. She works as a project manager in construction at UCLA and lives in Santa Monica.

Wendy Rainey is a student at California State University Long Beach, and has been previously published in *Tsunami* and *A Natural Force.*

Wendy Blumberg writes poetry, studies metaphysics and nutrition, works in her garden, enjoys the company of her family and friends. "I also think about the state of the world, especially our country, and from my own life, send thoughts of love and hope and peace to everyone. And everything. Everywhere.

Annie Boland now lives in New York.

Craig Borevitz is a poet/musician living and performing in Los Angeles. He has been published in *The Shattersheet, Impetus,* and *Saturday Afternoon.* He is also a member of California Poets in the Schools.

Eve Brandstein is a professional producer, director and writer for television, film and theatre. She has also been an educator, photographer and journalist. Born in Czechoslovakia, raised in the Bronx, N.Y., traveled throughout Europe and the Middle East, she presently lives in Los Angeles and is one of the directors of *Poets in Motion.* She is also the author of the book *The Actor—A Professional Guide to a Professional Career.*

Bob Brown has attended and has taught in many schools in Michigan where he was born; in Pennsylvania where he became a sculptor; and in California where he became a poet. He has just retired from teaching to become a full-time sculptor in Boulder Creek, near Santa Cruz, where he lives with his wife, Judy Dykstra.

Macdonald Carey is best known as Dr. Tom Horton in "Days of Our Lives," and for his work in over 60 films and several Broadway plays. He's been writing poetry most of his life and his first collection of poems, *A Day in the Life* was published by Coward McCann. In 1987 Bombshelter Press published *That Further Hill,* and *Beyond That Further Hill* was just published by The University of South Carolina Press. St. Martin's Press will be bringing out his autobiography *The Days of My Life.*

Mary Carden has written five books of poetry, and edited four anthologies of student poetry. Her work has appeared in *Poetry/LA, Tsunami,* and *ONTHEBUS.* She's given readings at the Bowers Museum and The Sculpture Gardens.

Jane Autenrieth Chapman was born in Indiana and has a master's degree in languages from Purdue University. She teaches German at Moorpark College in Moorpark, California and lives in Westlake Village with her husband, a daughter, 19, and a son, 16. Her poems have appeared in *Crosscurrents, Colorado-North Review,* and *Poetry/LA.*

Dori Denning grew up in Kansas and worked as a social worker in Kansas and Colorado before moving to Los Angeles in 1980. She now works as a marketing coordinator for a computer and printer manufacturer, but her true passions are writing, environmental causes and the outdoors.

Jane Dibbell is a collaborative performance artist. Some of the works she has presented in Southern California include *Sinatra Meets Max,* and most recently, *Passing Through* (performed at LATC, Sushi Gallery, and Claremont Graduate School). She is a college instructor in speech/drama, an actress, member of California Poets in the Schools, and mother of Julian (24) and Dominique (23).

Barbara Dube has been Los Angeles Coordinator for California Poets in the Schools, and was Founder/Director of The Writing Center at Cal State L.A. She is currently working on her dissertation.

Judy Dykstra-Brown was born in South Dakota and has lived in Australia, Ethiopia and Wyoming before coming to reside in Los Angeles. She now lives in Boulder Creek, California with her husband Bob and daughter Jodie.

ellen's poetry has been published in a number of journals and magazines, most recently in *Blue Window, Green Fuse, Poetry/LA, Blue Unicorn, ONTHEBUS,* and others. She has given many readings in the South Bay area and is listed in the *Directory of American Poets and Fiction Writers.*

Ruth Fineshriber was born in New York City, and has had a long career starting as a painter, then as director of her own gallery featuring the Surrealist painters, Magritte, Giacometti, Brauner, Masson, Matta and others. She completed her graduate studies in 1959 at the Institute of Fine Arts, New York University, which collaborated for the first time with the Metropolitan Museum of Art to offer the Master's Degree in Connoisseurship and Museum Training.

Cheri Gibson has been published in *Earthwise, ONTHEBUS,* and *Tsunami.* She read as a featured poet at Miller's Cafe, Gasoline Alley, Poecentric Lounge, and Be-Bop Records. During the 1989 Los Angeles Poetry Festival, she was featured in the New Voices segment and has been heard on KXLU, a local radio station, on a program featuring poetry with social and political themes.

Lisa Glatt was born in 1963 in Philadelphia, and grew up in Southern California. She studied English at the University of Hawaii, where in 1984 she received a Meryl Clark creative writing award. In Hawaii, she studied with Frank Stewart and Gene Frumkin. Lisa is currently living in Newport Beach, attending Long Beach State University and working on a new manuscript of poems tentatively titled *Toothpaste Moon.* Her poems and stories have appeared in *Pinchpenny, AKA Magazine, Pearl,* and *Tsunami.*

Connie Hershey runs a small publishing company, Artifact Press, in Concord, Massachusetts. After six years in L.A., she moved with her filmaker husband and four children to a country house overlooking the Sudbury River.

Valerie Johns is a college student and occasional comedy and screenwriter. Her work has appeared in *Vol. No.* and has been rejected by the *New Yorker.*

Debra Josephson is a performance poet. She brings her work to the stage with music, dance and theatrical effects. She has performed successfully in England and Los Angeles. A manuscript of poems, *From Earth and Back Again,* is currently seeking publication.

Jennifer M. Lanzilotta was born and raised in the Bronx, N.Y., and has lived in Los Angeles since 1984. She received a BA in English from City College of New York and a Masters in Education from Loyola Marymount University, Los Angeles. After teaching for five years she began working in the computer industry where she is a marketing professional. She is currently conducting her own writing support group for women. Her manuscript, *The Moments Between,* has just been completed.

Priscilla Lepera was one of the founding editors of *Tsunami,* a semi-annual poetry magazine.

Mona Locke's first poems, stories and artworks were published in the children's section of the *Oakland Tribune* when she was 12 years old. Since then, her credits include more than 60 articles and features published in newspapers and magazines, a supplemental college text, and work as writer/editor for several newsletters and brochures.

Barbara Lombardo lives in Mt. Baldy and teaches creative writing to Pomona nursing home residents, ages 18 to 102. Her work has previously been published in *ONTHEBUS.*

Cathleen Long received her B.A. in English—with Honors in Liberal Arts and Highest Distinction in English—from the University of Illinois, and her M.A. in English Language and Literature from the University of Chicago. Since 1979, she has been a full-time Instructor in English at Santa Monica College, having taught Creative Writing, Writing Fundamentals, and Literature, including specialized courses in the literature of D.H. Lawrence and Thomas Hardy. Her poetry has appeared in *Pandemonium,* and *Poetry/LA.* She has given readings in the L.A. and Bay areas, and is currently under contract with Holt, Rinehart, and Winston of New York to co-author a college writing text. With Jim Krusoe, she helped plan the first SMC Summer Writers' Conference for the L.A. writing community held at Santa Monica College in June of 1987.

Shirely Love has had poetry published in *Poetry/LA, Blue Unicorn, Tsunami,* and *Sculpture Gardens Review. She is also an associate editor of the Sculpture Gardens Review.*

Annette Lynch, college teacher, anthologized in *Fine Frenzy, Alone Amid All This Noise, Heart of the Matter,* Honorary Guest Poet: *Pomona Valley Collection,* and included in *California Poetry Quarterlies, Poem, University of Alabama, Wide Open, Mind's Eye, De Indo,* etc. A collection of her works has just been published by Lithe Press, titled *Ways Around the Heart.*

Anne Marple, a prose writer with awards from *Everywomen, Mademoiselle, Vogue,* and *Saturday Review,* began writing poetry 13 years ago. The first prize winner in *Blue Unicorn's* 1985 contest, she has published poems in *Cat Magazine, Green's Magazine, Gramercy Review, CQ, Light Year 1986, Amaryllis, Blue Window,* and the first 12 issues of *Poetry/LA.*

Ruben Martinez is a poet, journalist, and literary translator. He is also a staff writer for the *L.A. Weekley.* His approach to writing concerns itself with the cross-cultural hybridization of history, politics and philosophy in contemporary life.

Jill Moses is a Los Angeles poet from Atlantic City, New Jersey, who just moved from Salem, Oregon—where she worked on her MFA—to the University of Virginia where she will be teaching. She has read at the Sculpture Gardens in Venice, and won honorable mention in the 1986 Passaic County Poetry Center contest. While in Oregon she worked on the magazine *Poetry Northwest,* and started a poetry "school" called "Jewish Surrealism." How this will transfer to Virginia she isn't sure, but is working on a series of poems on Diane Arbus, the photographer, just in case.

Linda Neal is a writer and therapist, born and raised in Manhattan Beach, who vacations in her bedroom, The Northwest, and The Southwest. She's looking to get out of the city snarl on a more permenant basis in the near future. She is mother to two grown sons and a female Bernese Mountain Dog. The dog is house trained; the boys are not.

Ardis Nishikawa was born and raised in Los Angeles. She has a BA in American Studies from California State University, L.A. and an MA in Aging from North Texas State University. Her other publication is a paper on Multicultural Training in Senior Centers. She is co-publisher and co-editor of *Tsunami,* a poetry magazine.

Debra Pearlstein is a transplanted Bostonian now living in L.A. She attended Brown University where she majored in Semiotics (Communications and Creative Writing). After working in Book Publishing for three years, she spent a year in Paris studying at the Sorbonne, then traveled through Europe spending a summer on the island of Naxos, Greece. Her work has appeared in *Cosmopolitan, The Moment, Poetry/LA,* and *Women for All Seasons,* an anthology published by The Women's Building.

Mima Pereira has been writing poetry for about ten years. Her poems appear frequently in *Poetry/LA,* and in *Tsunami* and *Sculpture Gardens Review* where one of her poems, "Apples," won an honorable mention in the Ann Stanford Memorial Contest.

Wendy Rainey is a student at California State University Long Beach, and has published in *Tsunami* and *A Natural Force.*

Annie Reiner is a Los Angeles poet, painter, and playwright. Her poems have appeared in various literary magazines, and the recently published anthology, *Snow Summits in the Sun.* Two of her short stories recently won awards in the Greenfeather Press 1988 Fiction Competition. She has had several one-woman shows of her paintings and is currently preparing a book of poetry to be published by Momentum Press.

Jo Ellen Passman's work has appeared in *Shattersheet, Tsunami, St. Andrews Review, The Yellow Magazine, Aurora,* and *ONTHEBUS.*

Lee Rossi is editor of *Tsunami* magazine. He has been published in *Wormwood Review, The Jacaranda Review, Poetry/LA, Shattersheet, Tsunami, ONTHEBUS,* and *Blue Window.* He ran the Gasoline Alley poetry reading series, which has moved to a new location. He currently works in the computer industry in Southern California.

Joyce B. Schwartz has published poetry and articles in *CQ (California State Poetry Quarterly), The Gramercy Review, Green's Magazine, Response, Vol. No., Shattersheet, Seventeen, Writer's West, Fiber Arts, Womankind, Xerox Educational Publications, The Jewish Spectator,* etc. She is a featured poet in the anthology *Contents Under Pressure.* She's plugging away at a novel, coordinates the Sculpture Gardens Poetry Series at Venice Place, CA., and is editor of *The Sculpture Gardens Review.*

Leah Schweitzer's work appears in *The Small Press Review, The California State Poetry Quarterly, Apalacee Quarterly, Crosscurrents, Shattersheet, Bitterroot,* and *Israel Today.* She conducts creative writing workshops, and is an editor/writing consultant. Leah studied with Anais Nin, and attended Immaculate Heart College. She is currently co-editing *The Lion Whose Mane I Groom,* a collection of poetry about Israel.

Nan Sherman is a staff consultant at the Women's Center, sponsored by the National Council of Jewish Women. She has been an actress on the Broadway stage and began writing in 1981. Her poems haver appeared in several dozen literary magazines including *Pulpsmith, Piedmont Literary Review, Pegasus, Unicorn, Poetic Justice, Black Bear,* and *California State Poetry Quarterly.*

Shoshanna has been writing poetry since the age of eight. It is only recently, at the age of 42, that she has made a committment to honor the creative side of herself, her nightmares, dreams, and bout with cancer.

Laura Slapikoff has been published in *Lemon Fingers Emerge,* and *Shattersheet.*

Agnieszka Maria Soltysik was born in Warsaw, Poland in 1968, and spent part of her childhood there. She also lived in Montreal, Quebec, where she first began writing poems. She almost published a book in Canada called *Words, and More Words*. Presently, she's living in Los Angeles, and studying literature and Spanish.

Terry Blake Stevenson is an Assistant City Attorney for the City of Burbank. His poems have appeared in *Electrum, Poetry/LA*, and three anthologies — *Shards, Off-Ramp*, and *Corners*, published by the Pasadena Poets. More are forthcoming in a new anthology to be published by the same press later this year.

Herb Stout was a Deputy D.A. for the County of Los Angeles and is in private practice. He is a Veteran of Foreign Wars, having served in the 11th Airborne Division, 503rd Parachute Regiment.

Sita Stulberg is a poet, teacher and author whose work has appeared in *The Open Eye Poetry Journal, ONTHEBUS*, and *Dysfunction Magazine*. She founded The Inner Voice Poetry Series in Eugene, Oregon in 1987, and currently teaches in L.A. with California Poets in the Schools. Her books include *Before the Swan, Spare Change & Fist-Chested Women*, and *Listening for Eternity*.

Paula Thompson's poems have appeared in *The Sculpture Gardens Review, Blue Window, Shattersheet, Tsunami*, and *The Sand & Sea Anthology*.

Carol Bridge Walker has completed her internship in marriage, family and child counseling. Her poetry has appeared in *Poetry/LA, Southern Humanities Review, The Laurel Review, Blue Unicorn, Crosscurrents, Embers, Tinderbox* and *Poets' Voices 1984*.

Betsey Warwick is a medical editor with the Audio Digest Foundation in Glendale, California. She has had her poetry published in numerous small presses.

Florence Weinberger is a native of New York City, graduate of Hunter College, former teacher, former consumer advocate, former legal investigator. She is married and the mother of two daughters. Her poetry and fiction have been translated in numerous literary magazines, among them *Poetry/LA, Numrod, Calyx, Blue Window, Blue Unicorn, California State Poetry Quarterly, Cache Review, Friday, The Smith*, and *Fedora*. Two poems will appear in a forthcoming anthology, *Blood to Remember...American Poets on the Holocaust*. She has given frequent readings and was interviewed on KPFK's The Poetry Connection by Wanda Coleman and Austin Strauss.

Janet Wells, an honors graduate of UCLA, is an International Marketing Director of Insta Graphic Systems. She has lived in France and Germany, and has traveled extensively around the world.

Danella Wild lives in Redondo Beach. A working journalist for more than 20 years, she covers crime for United Press International. A chapbook, *Unclaimed Dreams*, was published last year.

Michele Williams, a junior high school assistant principal, has taught writing and poetry for years, and had a summer fellowship in the UCLA Writing Project.

Mary Lee Wilson started writing poetry about two years ago. Her first pregnancy and her first poems seemed to coincide. "If you believe in souls, maybe that explains it. Or maybe just hormones." She's never published anything except an article in the *Journal of Pediatrics*, titled "Myoglobinuria in the Newborn."

ONTHEBUS

A New Literary Magazine

The premiere Los Angeles literary quarterly that features the best in poetry, fiction, reviews, essays, & translations from around the world. Each issue highlighted by color reproductions from prominent artists and photographers.

FOURTH ISSUE

Volume 1, Number 4
Winter, 1989

INTERVIEWS WITH
Allen Ginsberg & William Burroughs

POEMS & PHOTOGRAPHS
Michael Andrews

POEMS & PROSE
Charles Bukowski • Ernesto Cardenal • Robert Peters • Ottó Orban
Stephen Dobyns • Lyn Lifshin • Richard Jones • Steve Kowit
Dallas Wiebe • Gerald Locklin • Jana Harris

REVIEWS
Another Path to the Waterfall by Raymond Carver
The River Of Heaven by Garrett Hongo
Night Parade by Edward Hirsch
Paradise Poems by Gerald Stern
Groom Falconer by Norman Dubie

Single Issue $8 (plus $1 postage)
One Year Subscription (4 issues): $24
❑ Begin with Issue 4.
❑ Begin with Issue 5.

BOMBSHELTER PRESS   6421½ Orange St., L.A., CA 90048

THE POET
FROM
THE CITY OF THE ANGELS
Poems and Photographs: 1969 to 1989
by
Michael Andrews

Forthcoming February 1990
Approximately 240 pages, including 35 color photographs.
ISBN 0-941017-16-8 $19.95

The Poet From The City Of The Angels will contain poems and photographs from the *Riding South*, *RiverRun* and *Machu Picchu* portfolios; selections from previous books and exhibits including *Gnomes and The Xmas Kid*, *Cityscapes and Naked Ladies* and *A Telegram Unsigned*, and also uncollected work from the High Sierras, Vietnam and Iran.

"**Michael Andrews** drives with his camera and his motorcycle into the very soul of the soul of his depth. He sees the secret wounds of pain. Michael Andrews, who carries his California strapped on his shoulders, who takes along with him his LA as Achilles his heel, is looking through his photographs for the other frontier. He brings with him the biting lyricism of the true poets of California. Michael Andrews the Gringo, the man from the Lost North and the Far West, follows the route away from the gods of his civilization, defies them to come with him, finds them in parking lots and cantinas transformed into plumed serpents and smoking mirrors, drives on. Beyond, there is the language of poetry, riddle and myth."

Carlos Fuentes

See a portfolio of photographs and poems in ONTHEBUS 4

BOMBSHELTER PRESS   6421½ **Orange Street, L.A., CA 90048**

Trees, Coffee, and the Eyes of Deer

New & Selected Poems

by

Jack Grapes

Jack Grapes is the author of 8½ books of poetry and a recipient of a Fellowship in Literature from the National Endowment for the Arts. He teaches poetry as part of the UCLA Extension program and is on the board of directors of California Poets in the Schools. He has received seven Artist-in-Resident grants from the California Arts Council. He is also an actor and playwright, having appeared in numerous plays and TV shows. He co-authored and starred in *Circle of Will*, a "bizarre metaphysical comedy" about Shakespeare's lost years.

"Grapes speaks for the extraordinary in the ordinary, for the life in old shoes, the overcoat you didn't hang up, for whatever life, humanity, possibility that can come from chaos. In his work and in his presentation of himself, a surface geniality frequently masks something dark and bloody. This flip-flop from genial buffoonery to commandant of the dark side seems paradigmatic of Grapes' approach to poetry."
Nancy Shiffrin, *Los Angeles Times*

"His language is common speech, heightened and confined through poetic skill and insight. It is not only easy to read, it reaches out for you. He manages to be levelheaded in building his poems, wonderfully and purposefully vague in atmosphere, while at the same time, making his points assuredly. It is difficult to explain and equally hard to delineate. It is the work's magic. Finally, Jack Grapes makes sense, and how many poets consistently do? His work is generous, passionate, as full-bodied as a meal and yet delicate as a fog, something which never falls between him and his writing, between his work and us. This unique usage of poetry, this humane artistic ideal, conscious or unconscious, of what poetry should be, is his own. Ours too, if we let it."
Dennis Cooper, *Bachy*

ISBN 0-941017-08-7 • 160 pages, $11.50
BOMBSHELTER PRESS 6421½ Orange Street, L.A., CA 90048

Poet from City of Angels by Michael Andrews. 240 pages, $18.50
That Further Hill by Macdonald Carey. 36 pages. 5.95
The Border by K. Harer, L. Cohen, & K. Shantiris. 52 pages. 4.95
Hidden Proofs by Bill Mohr. 68 pages. 4.95
Trees, Coffee, and the Eyes of Deer by Jack Grapes. 140 pages. 11.50
Scattered Light by Doraine Poretz. 32 pages. 4.95
Gnomes by Michael Andrews. 62 pages. 4.95
Offshoots by Shael Herman. 76 pages. 5.00
!Presto! by Jack Grapes & Vern Maxam. 16 pages. . . 3.00
Sea Marks by Michael Andrews. 16 pages. 3.00
History of the World by James Krusoe. 92 pages. . . . 8.00
History of the World, original cover by Michael Woodcock . 15.00
New Los Angeles Poets, ed. Jack Grapes. 200 pages. . . 12.50

THE ALLEY CAT READINGS,   Set of five: $75

From November 1975 to September of 1976, 5 anthologies of poetry were published to coincide with readings held at the Alley Cat Restuarant in Hermosa Beach. These anthologies are beautifully printed and designed and were printed in limited editions, featuring the best poets in Los Angeles.

Vol 1. Kate Braverman, James Krusoe, Doraine Poretz, Michael Andrews,
    Dennis Ellman, Michael C. Ford, Eloise Klein Healy, & Jack Grapes $50
Vol 2. Wanda Coleman, Barry Simons, Deena Metzger, Doraine Poretz,
    Michael Andrews, Michael C. Ford, & Ron Koertge $10
Vol 3. Michael Tracy (Woodcock), Kate Braverman, Bob Flanagan,
    John Thomas, Ben Pleasants, Carol Lewis, Jack Grapes, & Joseph Hansen $10
Vol 4. Features art and photographs by Dick Miller & Hella Hammid, and poetry
    by Bob Greenfield, Chris Desjardins, Bill Mohr, Roger Taus, Nancy Shiffrin,
    Carol Marsh, David Schulman, Kita Shantiris, James Krusoe, Linda Backlund,
    Jack Grapes, Doraine Poretz, Dennis Holt and a rare centerfold photograph of
    Marilyn Monroe at 16 $10
Vol 5. Dennis Ellman, Steve Richmond, Kita Shantiris, Michael Andrews,
    Doraine Poretz, Curtis Lyle, Eloise Klein Healy, Clark McCann. $10
    with original B&W photo as cover inset $50
    with original cibachrome color photo as inset $75
Complete Standard Set $75

Back issues of **ONTHEBUS**: First Issue $5 • Second Issue $7

ORDER INFORMATION

Individuals

You may order books directly from Bombshelter Press, 6421½ Orange Street, Los Angeles, CA 90048. Enclose payment with postage and handling charges of $1.25 for the first book and $.50 for each additonal book. CA residents add local sales tax. Allow from two to four weeks for delivery.

BOMBSHELTER PRESS

6421½ Orange Street, Los Angeles, CA 90048